Emotional Intelligence for Leadership

The Ultimate Guide to Improve Your Ability to Manage People and Your Social Skills. Boost Your EQ, Self-Discipline and Self Confidence (EQ 2.0)

William Cooper

professional before attempting any techniques outlined in this book.

By reading this document, the reader agrees that under no circumstances is the author responsible for any losses, direct or indirect, which are incurred as a result of the use of information contained within this document, including, but not limited to, — errors, omissions, or inaccuracies.

Table of Contents

Introduction

Congratulations on purchasing *Emotional Intelligence for Leadership: The Ultimate Guide to Improve Your Ability to Manage People and Your Social Skills. Boost Your EQ, Self-Discipline and Self Confidence (EQ 2.0),* and thank you for doing so.

It is my utmost desire to help you find the skills within yourself that you already possess to be the most effective leader possible. Today there is definitely a shortage of great leadership in the world and in the workplace, but with this book, you will find everything you need to increase your emotional intelligence and be the leader you have always wanted for yourself and others.

By learning exactly what emotional intelligence is, the five components of it, the history of the psychological study of it, plus practical applications that will help you increase your emotional intelligence, you will be ready to move on to applying it to leadership.

You will learn about the different types and styles of leadership, the effectiveness of each kind, the different approaches you can take to be most productive based on each style, as well as the number one desired leadership style and steps to take on how you can become the best type of leader there is, no matter what your current style.

You will also learn many of the most effective traits of great leaders, ways to communicate more efficiently and appropriately, plus many of the secret clues great leaders exude oh, so you can harness your own power. Finally, you will also learn many of the pitfalls that are very common amongst leaders, so you can be prepared for their lures and avoid them.

There are plenty of books on this subject on the market, thanks again for choosing this one! Every effort was made to ensure it is full of as much useful information as possible. Please enjoy!

Chapter 1
What Is Emotional Intelligence?

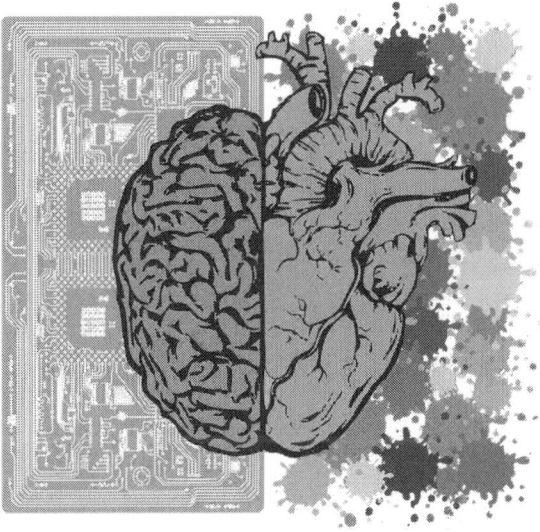

Defining Emotional Intelligence

So, what exactly is emotional intelligence? Emotional intelligence is the ability of a person to know and understand the emotions that they have, the emotions other people have, the ability to tell the difference between emotions, accurately named them, use that knowledge to affect how they think and behave, and deal with does emotions in order to successfully accommodate the situations they are in.

That may sound like a lot, but in reality, this is something almost every single person does most waking moments of their lives. You are a complex and nuanced human being who absolutely can do all of this, and in fact, already does it. Most people do this without any thought at all. All-day, every day, whenever you come in contact with another person, you are most likely using your emotional intelligence to navigate that interaction. Whether it's making a purchase at a checkout counter or going on a date, you are probably using your emotional intelligence to gather information about how you think the other person is feeling and, therefore, how you should communicate with them to have your ideal interaction.

Some ways that you might recognize high levels of emotional intelligence is in a person's ability to respond well when other people are being emotional, they have an innate sense of self worse, they are people you can trust, they take responsibility for themselves, they are able to deal with change, they are not especially impulsive, they are open-minded, they have a healthy level of ambition, they have in groups that they are a part of, they have initiative, they have a healthy level of optimism, they are sensitive and considerate to others, they work well with others, and they know how to work toward a goal.

These are all skills that translate and are present in all aspects of a person's life, from professional relationships to familial and personal relationships.

The Ability Model

One way that we understand the development of emotional intelligence is through a communication model based on the person's ability. This basically means that when scientists try to study the development of emotional intelligence, they noticed that some aspects could be measured, and those measurements directly correlated to how successful or unsuccessful a person was at developing emotional intelligence.

The ability model can be explained in four parts:
A person's ability to perceive emotions. If you are able to see another person, even just a photograph, and recognize the emotion, they are portraying, that is a crucial element in being able to develop emotional intelligence. This also includes a person's ability to perceive their own emotions. This may take the shape of recognizing changes and yourself, knowing that this is an emotion, and then also being able to accurately label that emotion.

A person's ability to use emotions. If you can recognize the emotions you are having and appropriately use those to succeed in a situation. This is a huge determining factor in your ability to develop emotional intelligence. To know that your emotions can assist you in achieving tasks, problem-solve, or think more clearly is a measure of intelligence.

A person's ability to understand emotions. This includes the knowledge that some emotions are very similar to others, and therefore some nuances indicate the differences. This also encapsulates the advanced understanding that certain emotions can naturally lead to other emotions in a type of evolution.

A person's ability to manage emotions. This includes managing both their own emotions as well as those in other people. Not to be confused with controlling, but rather recognizing that you affect other people.

The Trait Model

This model of understanding emotional intelligence is based on how people perceive themselves. The way this is constructed and measured is based on how a person reports their own perception of themselves in a survey or questionnaire.

Not unlike personality quizzes, this model of understanding emotional intelligence is formulated through questions where people rate themselves on certain emotional skills and competencies. These are questions such as, "how well do you recognize anger in another person?" with answers usually ranging along a scale from "not very well at all" to "very well."

The Mixed Model

This model is based on 5 skills of emotional intelligence that can be acquired and improved upon. This is in contrast to the ability model, which assumes a type of knowledge that cannot be changed within a person. This is also in contrast to the trait model, which is an unreliable collection of data due to the participants' own self-reporting.

This combines both a person's naturally born capability along with their own understanding of themselves and their ability to learn and grow.

Goleman's Emotional Intelligence Framework

Daniel Goleman is a psychologist and journalist who studies the intersection of psychological thought and business. In his work, he wrote a book called Emotional Intelligence. In it, he hypothesized that emotional intelligence was a combination of both innate abilities and learned competencies that could be improved upon. The mixed model theory is his creation that's he put forth in his book.

He suggested that five components go into making up a person's emotional intelligence: self-awareness, Self-regulation, motivation, empathy, and social skills. These will be discussed in detail in chapter 4 of this book.

He goes on to explain that these competencies all depend upon each other as well as increase the success and advancement of the others when one increases in one area.

What Is Emotional Intelligence for Leadership

Emotional intelligence for leadership is something that is often severely lacking, but most people assume is very common. There are leaders and managers in every industry and at every level. How they got there, however, may or may not have anything to do with their emotional intelligence.

The best leaders have a high level of emotional intelligence, but that does not necessarily mean that the leaders we think of as being the most successful are truly the best. Rather than being a caricature of a high-functioning sociopath who takes no consideration of other people into account when making business decisions, this book argues that a type of leadership that is very considerate of the group's emotions will produce not only more positive feelings but also more successful financially.

Daniel Goleman's Work

Throughout more of his work, Goleman focused specifically on the applications of emotional intelligence to leaders in business. He argues that the best leaders have a high level of emotional intelligence to successfully create a team atmosphere that improves social skills, harnesses positive internal motivation, and utilizes empathy in group settings.

He puts forth that great leaders have a way of combining both the emotional constraints that all humans feel along with the logical decision-making part of our brains. A leader's ability to way both of those with both empathy and effectiveness is how they instill Trust in their employees. Because a leader's ability to empathize with the people they are leading is necessary to understand how and why they act the way they act, even so far as to predict how they will act, is an element many failed leaders are lacking in.

Chapter 2
A Brief History of Emotional Intelligence

History

For as long as humans have been attempting to pass along and knowledge to Future Generations, there has been an understanding that emotions are an important thing to master. Not only that, but they are crucial to every element of our lives, and managing them is important to mastering every other aspect of our life. In fact, it can be argued that the oral traditions of ancient philosophers from across the globe were actually explaining the importance of emotional intelligence back then.

As early as the 1930s, psychologists recognized specifically the importance of a person's ability to interact socially in the world in their ability to lead successful lives. They found that human interaction is critical to human life, and it is inextricable from all other elements of a person's daily life. This means that you cannot compartmentalize aspects of your life, such as knowledge, physical ability, emotions, and social interactions. They are all related to and affect one another. That finding was expounded upon in the 1940s as well. Then, in the 1950s, it was discovered that a person's emotional strength is something that could be built upon and improved, rather than being a static and unchanging element of their personality.

In the mid-1900s, when there was a resurgence of interest in Psychology and attempting to study the unknown realm of our heads and our hearts, a lot of scientists put work into trying to classify and better understand our emotions. It was at this time that a true scientific Paradigm was put on the importance of studying emotions. In fact, it was in the 1970s that the concept of having different types of intelligence was first introduced.

Rather than simply having the one emotional quotient that we are all familiar with, it was suggested that everyone has many types of intelligence, such as musical ability, control over their body, and interpersonal intelligence, among other things.

While the phrase emotional intelligence was first coins in the publication in the 1960s and used sporadically for the next couple of decades after that, it wasn't until the 1990s that the term came into the general Public's consciousness thanks to Daniel Goleman's work. Since then, there has been a general consensus of understanding about what emotional intelligence means and its alter egos such as EQ, being a play on IQ, and emotional intelligence quotient.

Disagreements

Of course, as with all studies of science, there has been some disagreement over exactly what emotional intelligence is, how we should define it, how we should determine what it is, and how we should measure it. The three models mentioned in chapter one is just one example of how different views codify their different interpretations of EQ.

Similarly, others argue that emotional intelligence is not even a type of intelligence at all. Because it is something that you can improve upon, some people argue that it is a skill, not unlike the ability to play a musical instrument or draw a picture. On a related note, a person's knowledge of how they should act in a particular interaction does not mean that they can or will act that way. This means that it is a theoretical knowledge rather than a practical one, which calls into question the use of it.

Others complain that our current perceptions of emotional intelligence are based on current moral Norms that change over time and are inherently biased toward fitting in with currently accepted Society. The measuring tool is that of comparisons to others, which emphasizes conforming to the larger group, rather than a true north, which is impossible to gauge. Specifically, when used inappropriately, the tools of developing High emotional intelligence can be used to manipulate others for negative reasons.

The most common refrain from naysayers of emotional intelligence is that the purpose of scientific hypotheses is usually to predict future behavior.

In the case of EQ, there is no ability to predict someone else's actions or emotions with the models and data we have acquired around emotional intelligence. This is especially true when considering the trait model where a person reports on themselves. This test can be easily gamed by a person with low emotional intelligence who perceives themselves to have high emotional intelligence, for instance.

Impact

When looking at the impact of the discovery and enumeration of emotional intelligence in the business world, however, you can see the massive influence it has had on promoting a human-centered approach to what has historically been a financial center industry. As more and more jobs become automated in the current market, the ability to connect on a human level is growing even more important. Most working adults today understand that their jobs are ones that require the knowledge that only a living human can offer, and they want to be seen as valuable to the organization.

Similarly, employers are soon going to find themselves with a labor shortage, which means they will need to do as much as they can to retain and attract good employees. To hold on to good personnel, many businesses and managers should look to improving their Leader's emotional intelligence. To stay relevant in the business industry, employees and employers can maximize their attractiveness by using the qualities that go along with high emotional intelligence.

In fact, one of the most human acts that we have in life and business is creativity and innovation. No matter how intelligently we design artificial computers to do our work for us, there is no alternative to the amount of evolution and outside of the box thinking human employees and leaders can provide. Especially when so many people leave emotional intelligence by the wayside as they increasingly isolate themselves using technology that allows them to participate in society without interacting with other people, a higher emotional intelligence will only become more valuable.

Chapter 3
EQ vs. IQ

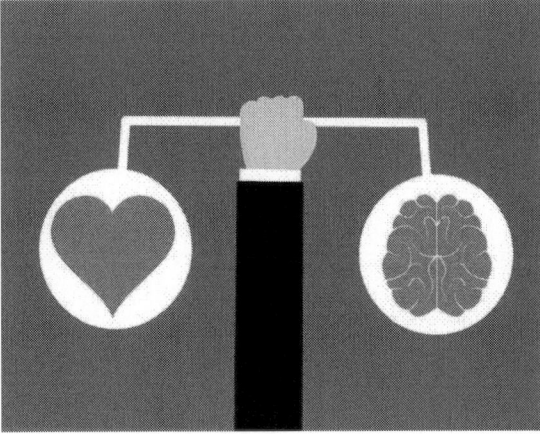

What Is IQ?

What exactly is IQ? An intelligent quotient is a score that reflects a person's ability to reason. Rather than measuring how smart a person is, it is actually a measurement of how well you could use logic, information, memory, and predictions to learn. An IQ test is actually comprised of multiple tests whose scores are generally averaged and then divided by a person's age.

With a range anywhere between 0 and 200, with the average being 100, a person's score is only compared to other people of the same age. For instance, the average child would have an IQ of 100, because their tests are created for children of their own age. Similarly, an average adult would also have an IQ of 100, rather than being compared to the intelligence of a child.

Developed by psychologists when commissioned by the French government to determine which students in school would have the hardest time. Interestingly, the Creator himself noted that this test failed to measure a person's creative ability or their knowledge of navigating social and emotional interactions.

Throughout the years, there have been many controversies and concerns surrounding the invention and use of an IQ test altogether. Because intelligence is so highly valued, be concerned about putting a numerical value of Intelligence on an individual has been seen as dehumanizing and short-sighted in determining the value of that person.

This can be seen in schools and professions that require a certain IQ score before accepting the person into their program. Other important issues relate to the inherent flaws of the tests do to the inherent flaws of the people who create them. Any internal biases the creators may have reflected in the test, resulting in biased scores for the test takers.

What Is EQ?

On the flip side, an emotional quotient is a score that reflects a person's ability to appropriately recognize and respond to their own and other people's emotions. Much like an IQ, it does not measure how good at emotions a person is; it rather measures how well you could use your knowledge to improve your recognition and responding to a motion.

Unlike an IQ, there are not any scientifically used IQ tests, but instead, there are many unofficial tests you can find online and in books. There is not a general consensus of how the scoring works, so there is no wide-sweeping understanding of what a high score is and what a low score is.

In fact, as discussed in chapter 1, there is not even one understood method of defining and measuring an EQ. for that reason, you will find many different definitions, models, tests, measurements, and results that all claim to explain emotional intelligence.

,on and Measurement

,he IQ test was invented and used at a governmental
a.. cial level, people consider it to be a professional and
undisputed way of measuring intelligence. As discussed
earlier, many people disagree with the test and its
methodology altogether. However, that does not dissuade
most of the general public from using an IQ score as a major
determining factor in how they view other people. Similarly,
it's Prevalence in pop culture and easy to understand
numerical score has given it a foothold in society that
convinces the general public that it is objective and
unquestionable.

On the flip side, the various attempts at explaining emotional
intelligence are far less commonplace or understood by most
people. For that reason, many people don't recognize it as
being as objective or studious as its intelligence counterpart.
As discussed in chapter one, The Trait model of measuring EQ
is especially quarrelsome, allowing for easy manipulation of
the results, whether intentional or not.

Which Is More Important?

As mentioned above, there has been a long history of valuing a high IQ in a person in a drastic amount in comparison to other aspects of the person and what they contribute to society. It was believed that the higher the IQ, the more successful they would be, and the more desirable they were as people, whether that is as a partner, employee, leader, or parent. An assumption was made that their high ability to use logic and reason to perform tests would lead directly to success in life, such as being ambitious, achieving high goals, and outperforming other people. Of course, we know now that this is not true.

A person's ability to perform does not prescribe that they will perform to that degree, or that they will be ambitious, outperform, or achieve any goals at all. While there is a correlation, that does not mean that a high IQ causes success in life.

There are many more factors at Play Then intelligence. Rather than being the main determining factor in a person's achievements, it is merely one component in a much larger machine.

Because of its controversial and varied approaches toward understanding emotional intelligence, there has been less mandated education and measuring of EQ. However, it has clearly been well understood for centuries that it is an important part of all of our lives, and the last century has given us enough scientific research to prove that to be true. For that reason, emotional intelligence has been often looked over when evaluating important aspects of measuring a successful life.

It is believed that a person's ability to use introspection to improve their emotional intelligence is a predictor and amplifier of all kinds of intelligence. It is the ability to consider your thoughts and emotions that will translate into a type of introspection and continued learning that will lead to many more successes throughout life.

Impact of Emotional Intelligence in Daily Life

Some of the biggest proponents for teaching and utilizing emotional intelligence is the massive impact it can have on everyone's daily life.

On a personal level, and applies to people of all ages, including children, is a very common concern about bullying. Because so much of our Lives now take place through technology rather than in face-to-face interactions, the prevalence of bullying has skyrocketed. Due to the perpetrator's physical and emotional distance, as well as their perception that they are anonymous, and there is a common understanding that they will not receive any repercussions. However, the level of emotional intelligence does seem to correlate with both a person's likelihood of becoming a bully, as well as a person's likelihood of being victimized by bullying behavior. In both instances, by introducing the competencies of emotional intelligence, you can help to prevent the bullying behavior, as well as minimizing the damage done to the victim.

There have been many studies that show that a person with higher emotional intelligence also correlates with higher mental and physical health. It shows that there is an understood connection between the importance of managing your own emotions and the similarities between managing your physical capacities and mental health. Specifically, an increase in emotional intelligence decreased the people's use of recreational drug and alcohol use.

In personal relationships, the use of emotional intelligence is very easily seen, but not as often utilized as it should be. The ability to recognize when someone is trustworthy is an important part of maintaining stable relationships, which then allow you to be open and vulnerable with them. This builds stronger bonds with them, which allows them the opportunity to help you at your most difficult moments. By creating deep bonds with others, we feel truly invested in our own lives, and it provides a sense of being truly seen and understood in the world.

Chapter 4
The Five Components of Emotional Intelligence

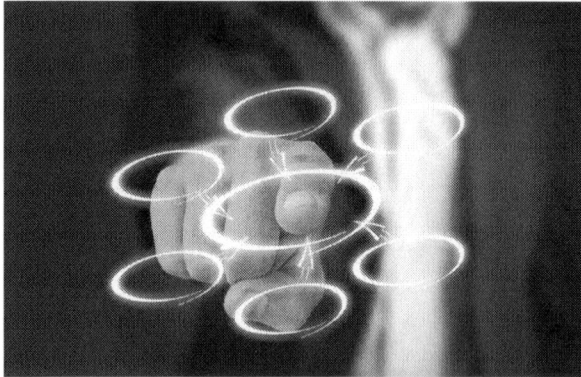

Five components go into making up emotional intelligence. These are important, and you cannot have emotional intelligence without each of them. There levels of an advanced understanding of all of these, and they all begin infancy and become more nuanced and better understood as you mature and age.

Self-Awareness

So, what exactly is self-awareness? It is being able to see and have an understanding of your own emotions that are happening inside of you, things that create a cause and effect on your emotions, things that trigger knee-jerk emotional responses and you, and how you were a presentation of your emotions affect the people around you.

There are a few ways that you can tell if your cell for another person has an appropriate level of self-awareness. A few things include if you have a reasonable amount of confidence in actions that you perform regularly and interactions you have had for a considerable amount of time. For instance, if you are friends with someone for 5 years, you should have a reasonable amount of confidence that that person truly is your friend, and they do not think negatively of you. Conversely, if you have been friends with someone for 5 years and you are constantly worried about their perception of you or if they are going to get mad at you over misunderstandings, this could show a low level of self-awareness.

Another way that you can tell if someone has a healthy level of self-awareness is how harshly they treat themselves for mistakes. Of course, we are all human, so we all make small mistakes from time to time, which usually causes little to no harm whatsoever. However, if you have difficulty separating big mistakes from small mistakes or beat yourself up over insignificant mistakes, there's a possibility that you have a low level of self-awareness.

Improving self-awareness gets easier as you grow older, as very small children have little to no understanding of their self, cognitively. However, you must spend some dedicated time being introspective to increase this. It is a conscious effort that everyone needs to take to recognize themselves and their effects on their world around them.

Self-Regulation

Self-regulation is the ability to deal with your own emotions and healthily process them. How that manifests itself is going to be different for every person and in every situation. However, it is important to note that the expression of emotion needs to be done in a healthy way. That means acting out in a harmful way is a regressed and unhelpful way to self-regulate. This also means that pretending that you do not have emotions is also a regressed and unhelpful way to self-regulate.

The ability to self-regulate your emotions is another aspect that is nearly impossible for infants but gets easier as you age and mature. That being said, there are absolutely ways that infants and small children learn to regulate their emotions. These are known as self-soothing techniques that allow them to calm themselves down when they are upset. For instance, if a baby is no longer in the presence of their parents, such as when they get put into bed for the night, a lot of infants will use some sort of security blanket, cuddle with a stuffed animal, suck on their thumb, or suck on a pacifier. All of these are examples of babies self-regulating their emotions, which is pretty amazing if you think about it.

As we grow older, hopefully, we learn more appropriate ways to regulate our own emotions. As our emotions become more complex and nuanced, we will need to learn new tactics and techniques to express ourselves. This will come to include not only the ability to self-soothe, but also stop and think rationally before taking any actions that are steeped in Emotion. It also means we will be able to recognize certain patterns we have to not be swept up in negative behaviors.

Motivation

Motivation is the reasoning behind an action or actions. It is why you are acting a certain way. When it comes to emotional intelligence, understanding your motivation and others' motivations is a complex and advanced art. Specifically, it has a reason to behave that goes beyond satisfying your ego. It is an internal force that tells you to keep calm and keep doing the right one else is to congrats or reward.

One thing this means is not being moved to action in hopes of receiving external rewards. Just like the idea of getting a huge paycheck, becoming famous, winning Awards, or getting personal recognition, all of these are usually desires of the ego. They come from outside of you and are completely dependent on other people telling you that you did the right thing. To be emotionally intelligent, you have to recognize these desires for what they are, and take action for reasons that you decide are important, rather than reasons that are important to others. When you prioritize your internal motivation, you will be more successful, happier, more committed, and have a better understanding of yourself.

Interestingly, this can also take the form of manipulation. If you were motivation is to get other people to do what you want them to do without consideration of their views on the matter, that is another form of external motivation. You are trying to control things outside of your purview. While this may get you what you want, it is not at all an emotionally intelligent way to go about it. In fact, rather than having a better understanding of yourself, you are ignoring your motivations and emotions deep down.

Empathy

Empathy is being able to understand and identify with other people's feelings. This means that you recognize other people's emotions and also recognize that you have felt that same emotion before. This is surprisingly, something that also begins with very young children. Of course, this will gets easier, and you will get better at it over time, but it has to be practiced.

This is a complex element of emotional intelligence because not only does it require that you recognize emotions in another person, but it also requires that you have felt that same emotion yourself.

For almost everyone, this is a natural progression of our emotional maturity. The way we recognize these things is first by taking stock of how you respond when you are feeling certain emotions. Most likely, you feel physical Sensations and have thoughts that occur when you are feeling emotional. There's also a good chance, especially as a child, that when you were acting emotionally, other people responded to you in a particular way depending on that emotion. For instance, if you were crying, someone probably came to check on you, ask how you are feeling, hug you, or help you feel better. You now associate those actions with that particular emotion. So, when you see someone else physically responding in a way that you recognize to be an indicator of an emotion, most likely, you will feel compelled to respond in the way that other people treated you in that instance.

The way this manifests itself is that with higher levels of empathy, you become more emotionally intelligent because you respond appropriately when other people are showing their emotions. This is done from a place of understanding and support, because you have also felt similarly, and you want to assist them, rather than acting with your own emotions in the Forefront.

Social Skills

The ability to have social interactions with other people is crucial to every single human development. This affects literally every aspect of a person's health, from physically, mentally, emotionally, to spiritually. This is also, obviously, something that begins even before we are born, and unless we intentionally become a Hermit coup hiding from society, it happens almost nearly 24 hours a day, 7 days a week, now with our new technologically connected culture.

A great thing about improving our social skills when it comes to emotional intelligence is that we are constantly getting practice with it. That being said, they're certainly could be more direction for those of us who find it difficult. Some ways that we normally learn to improve our social skills are simply by noticing how others respond to us and our actions, which then tells us whether or not they liked, approved, or appreciated us at that moment. Likely, we have learned behaviors is that elicited positive responses from the people around us because it makes us feel good when other people like us. However, as we grow older and more mature, we begin to differentiate between the people whose opinions of us are more important, in comparison to the people whose opinions of us do not matter much.

Interestingly, we also learn to adjust our social interactions based on many factors, such as where we are, who we are with, what we are doing, what time of day it is, as well as many other variables. This is something we do and learn our entire lives. Unfortunately, sometimes be behaviors we learn as a child to survive in that setting are based on unhealthy interactions with others. That means we learn patterns that will eventually create some sort of stumbling block in our future. Thankfully, we can change and improve our social skills at absolutely any age.

Chapter 5
Emotional Intelligence and Delaying Gratification

Example of Gratification Delay

You have most likely heard of the famous "marshmallow test" performed by a psychologist in the 1960s. It is well known for its simplistic nature yet important results it yielded. The experiment is that the scientists would place a marshmallow in front of a child and ask them not to eat it yet. Instead, if they could wait, they would get more marshmallows in a few minutes. The psychologist wanted to test and learn about children's abilities to delay gratification rather than succumb to the instant gratification that was sitting in front of them.

Of course, every child's reaction was different, some lasting mere seconds before eating their marshmallow, others were able to successfully wait the entire length of time. Many, however, whether successful or not, did attempt their own ways of managing the anxiety they felt about wanting to eat the marshmallow now but also wanting to follow the rules to get more marshmallows later. Much like self-soothing techniques, we begin to learn as children to manage our emotions; some of these children used techniques to attempt to increase their odds of success.

Some kids tried to look away or move away from the marshmallow so that their physical proximity wouldn't be as tempting. Other kids try to find ways to occupy themselves to keep their mind off of the very appealing marshmallow in front of them. These techniques were relatively successful but not always. On the flip side, some children try to distract themselves from eating the marshmallow by playing with the marshmallow, some wood poke it, squeeze it, or bat it between their hands. Unsurprisingly, these techniques were less successful in soothing the children's anxiety or distracting them. Because they were putting themselves in connection with the very thing they were trying to distract themselves from, they were more likely to eat the marshmallow.

Success and Delaying Gratification

While the results were definitely interesting as to how some children were able to delay gratification and how they did so, the truly informative part of the experiment was the follow-up research he did 10 years later. The psychologist followed up with all of the children who participated in that experiment 10 years down the road to determine if there was in any correlation or causation between their ability to delay gratification as a child and their continued success in their education and general well-being in life.

The tests showed that the children who were most successfully able to delay gratification with their marshmallows had higher test scores, better grades, fewer health problems, and were more socially Adept than their counterparts.

That is not all, however. The psychologists also followed up with those same children 40 years after the original marshmallow test, too, once again assess the long-term correlations and causation between delayed gratification as children and success as adults. Similarly, he found results that mirrored those found 30 years prior.

An interesting thing to note in the original marshmallow test, though, is that for some of the children who ate their marshmallow before the time was up, the scientist gave them some coaching to help them succeed with this experiment. Those children who were taught a technique to delay gratification fared even better than the children who did manage the original test on their own. In fact, the children who originally failed then were taught a lesson, before being given a second chance at the test were able to wait on average two times as long as the original test called for.

Both of these approaches toward delaying gratification end up being effective, whether a child or adult is innately born with a large amount of self-control or if they are encouraged and directed toward it externally. The great news is that anyone can acquire this skill, much like every other element of emotional intelligence. However, it is something that you have to be conscientious of, and only you can hold yourself responsible for learning and practicing to build this muscle.

Impulse Control and Delayed Gratification

So now that we understand the scientific backing between the connection of delayed gratification and success in life, how can we understand our impulse control to be successful? Actually, this is part of emotional intelligence. I desire you feel, no matter how intense or sudden, is simply an emotion that you are having. To overcome, you can apply the principles we discussed in chapter 4. This means you need to learn how to manage this emotion.

Of course, the ability to decide that long-term success is more powerful and important to you then an immediate desire is easier said than done. However, the ability to do so will have exponentially important results in every aspect of your life. The difference between the marshmallow test and your impulse control in day-to-day experiences are going to be drastic. The only person who can tell you if it even is a test of your impulse control is yourself, and you are held accountable to no one. On that same note, there are no Rewards or extra marshmallows for adults who manage their impulse control in everyday life.

Part of the necessary components to use your impulse control as an adult is to have a certain level of trust in your long-term success. In the experiment, the children trusted that the scientist would give them more marshmallows if they succeeded, as they said they would. In your own life, however, fuel rewards are as guaranteed as those extra marshmallows. Putting in extra time at work, for instance, isn't a guarantee for a promotion or raise. That means you have to have trust in the process, and the results of your efforts will be worth it.

Some ways to increase your success and impulse control are to apply strategies just like those children. In fact, a great way to delay gratification if something has suddenly appeared that you desire in the short-term, but no is not good for you in the long-term is to do just as they did and try to distract yourself. Perhaps you can physically separate yourself from it, turn your attention away from it, or even better, put your attention into something else that is consuming.

For other Temptations, give yourself a time frame, just as those scientists gave to the children. Maybe you cannot control your impulses forever, but surely you can control them for just 15 minutes. After those 15 minutes, chances are your brain has moved on to something else and will feel less tempted. Or, perhaps after those 15 minutes, you want to give yourself another 15 minutes.

Stop, Drop, Roll Technique

One great technique you can use to manage your impulse control to delay gratification is called the stop, drop, roll technique. Just like when you learned about fire safety as a child, these same words can help you as an adult in overwhelming impulse situations.

Stop

The first thing you should do when you feel as if you are about to make an impulsive decision is stopping yourself right in your tracks. Then in there, physically, and mentally take a moment to recognize that this is a situation that is triggered your desires. You cannot control your impulses if you do not recognize the moment when they are in control rather than your logical and rational part of your brain. Use this moment to think about what it is that you are feeling so impulsive about. What emotions are coming up? What actions do you want to take? How do you feel physically? Was there a lead up to this, or did this happen very suddenly? All of these can help you determine what you are feeling and help you in the future to prevent this overwhelming impulse.

Drop

Now that you understand what is happening to you, you need to start doing some critical thinking about the situation. Drop the very compelling story that your emotions are convincing you is real. Drop the desire that your endorphins have created. Drop the assumed gratification you think you will get from acting on this impulse. While all of those things feel very real at the moment, in reality, they are just figments of your desire's creation. If you can give yourself some time from them, in a few moments, you will see that they were fleeting rather than true desires.

Roll

Finally, after you have managed to stop amid your impulse taking over and drop the facade that it's created to tempt you, you can roll out your decision. If this is a behavior that you do repeatedly and after the fact, you wish you hadn't taken that action, this is your opportunity to break that pattern. Now that you have the space to think rationally about your impulses, you can decide if delaying gratification is what you truly want.

Self-Mastery Is Master Key

Just like every other aspect of emotional intelligence, the ability to self-mastery impulse control and delayed gratification is absolutely a tool that will serve you for the rest of your life as well as being a muscle that needs to be used and practiced to become strong. This requires your conscious effort and thought to be put into it. You must recognize the behaviors and patterns to break them. You must also understand yourself well enough to recognize your triggers to avoid them. It also demands that you have a relatively high level of emotional intelligence in all of the other components to be most successful. If you do not know what your long-term success looks like concerning an impulse, you will never be able to overcome it. That being said, you also need to have a level of empathy and understanding for yourself because you will fail sometimes, and that is okay. Self-mastery takes time and requires a level of balance, rather than complete abstinence or perfection.

Chapter 6
The Benefits of Emotional Intelligence

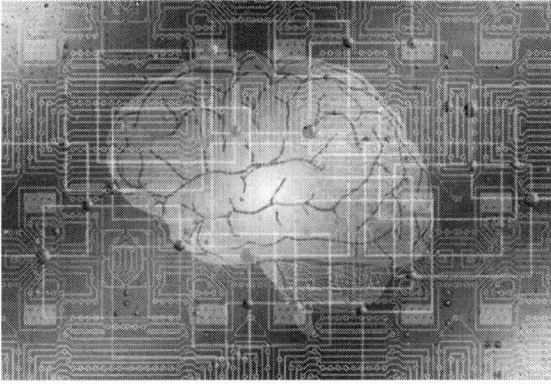

Conversation Skills

Part of improving emotional intelligence is not simply to improve yourself alone. Because none of us live in a vacuum, none of our emotional intelligence can occur without some outside influence, most likely with the people that we interact with every day. So not only will you be improving your emotional intelligence when you have conversations, but it is a continuous feedback loop that means that as your emotional intelligence increases, your conversation skills will also get better.

Studies show that communicators who have a higher emotional intelligence are exponentially more effective than those with a lower score. This is because a conversation is a two-way street that requires the participation of both people. That is done most successfully when both participants are considerate of the feedback and information the other is giving them. As we already know, the ability to manage our own emotions as well as those of others is an important component of emotional intelligence. That means that in conversations, we will be using this skill to better understand the person we are talking with as well as altering how we talked with them to best, and most clearly communicate the message we are trying to convey.

This can present itself in many ways. People with higher emotional intelligence can have more difficult conversations without getting as flustered or overwhelm as their counterparts. This is because they can take in the situation, recognize, and manage those difficult emotions very quickly on the spot, before using their impulse control, send social skills to tactfully navigate those conversations.

Another way this presents itself is in leaving the other person feeling as if they were heard and understood during the conversation. Because you have learned how to show and communicate empathy as well as recognizing the healthy internal motivation to have that conversation, it allows you to eliminate some of your ego and commit to listening and hearing out the other person.

People Skills

One of the most sought-after benefits of emotional intelligence is very ambiguous but decidedly important people skills. It is hard to nail down exactly what it is, but it is definitely something that exists and improves with higher emotional intelligence.

Perhaps one element of having good people skills is that you are authentically yourself when you are around other people. This is something emotional intelligence can help you bring to fruition because you have done enough internal work to recognize the truth about yourself and how best to present those two other people.

It also shows up because not only do you have empathy for other people, but you also have empathy for yourself and the difficult parts of yourself that you are still currently working on. Emotional intelligence helps you understand that you are a worthy and competent person who has something to gain by spending time with others; therefore, you know that your authentic self is the best version to put forth.

One way that this shows up is in maturity or level of assuredness in oneself. An emotionally intelligent person can show their improve people skills by the healthy relationships they have with others. Rather than seeing the world as a competition in which there can only be one winner, an emotionally intelligent person knows that they are not a victim, and there is no such thing as winning. Instead, everyone is winning in their way, and they are content with themselves and their journey in life. They have a worldview that is full of compassion for others as well as themselves, and therefore they are better able to connect with others.

Teamwork

Because emotional intelligence is so focused on navigating relationships with others, it only makes sense that people with higher emotional intelligence are also better at teamwork. This is because as difficult as it is to navigate the emotions and conversations with one other person when you are working on a team, you must do that same task but with every other person on the team, as well as the team as a whole.

The point of a team is almost always to accomplish some sort of goal together that wouldn't be able to be accomplished by just a single person. That means the team has a purpose for being together. As an emotionally intelligent person, you can recognize that this is an external motivation for the group. However, you also recognize that every individual has their own internal motivation for why they are participating. This knowledge can help you navigate any obstacles you may come up against as you work towards your goal.

A big part of the success of a team is dependent upon how engaged the members of the team feel in their work.

This means that as individuals, everyone wants to know that they are important, and their work is crucial to the team's success. If they are being micromanaged or do not have very much flexibility or empowerment when it comes to how they do their job, this can result in them feeling as if they shouldn't be a part of a team, or that their efforts are not good enough. As an emotionally intelligent team member, you can recognize this either before it starts or once it has already begun, and attempt to resolve this issue.

When members of the team have high emotional intelligence, this can improve engagement by encouraging team members to work together to succeed rather than feel competition with their peers. A way that this can manifest itself is in teammates communicating frequently, clearly, and positively toward each other, encouraging each other, and celebrating the completion of smaller goals that work toward the end goal.

Leadership Skills

Most importantly, a high emotional intelligence gives you such a leg up when it comes to being a leader. Because you are in a role in which you are in charge of your employees, and you assigned the tasks that they spend most of their day on, it absolutely matters how you treat them, how you support their work, and how you respond to them. It is well understood that a happy employee is a productive employee. Your ability to appropriately communicate and celebrate the accomplishments of your team will go a long way in improving your leadership skills.

Having higher emotional intelligence will not only help you understand why it's important to be respectful to your employees and co-workers, but it will instill in you an innate sense of respect for others. This is crucial to keeping your employees satisfied and engaged, which has a direct correlation to their participation and success in work.

It also improves your leadership skills because you are more able to quickly adapt and change on the Fly. I do not know of many leadership roles that have no sudden situations that have to be dealt with or fires that need to be put out.

Your ability to see the bigger picture, be aware of yourself and the team, regulate your own emotions and those of your team, and then implement a plan that keeps the long-term success in mind are all aspects of emotional intelligence.

Chapter 7
Emotional Intelligence in a Relationship

Communicate

A relationship is most basically just two people who have decided, but they are important to each other. One of the most simple and impactful ways we can show another person they are important to us is by communicating with them. Whether that is taking time out at the end of every day to tell each other about how their day went, to be available to each other when an important or a difficult occasion arises, being able to communicate with each other is a crucial part of a relationship.

This also helps when it comes to communicating about your relationship. This could mean having the "what are we?" conversation or "when should we have kids" discussion, and everything in between. What is important is that a relationship that is fulfilling has communicated boundaries and a shared vision. The only way you can achieve those is with a high level of emotionally Intelligent Communication.

It has also been shown that Partners who have engaging conversations with each other have a higher level of satisfaction in those relationships. This can be encouraged by participating in events together; that way, you have something to talk about. Specifically, trying something new to both of you together is very effective in creating not only new topics of conversation but also closer feelings of trust.

Empathy

When in a relationship with another person, you both must know that you are there for each other, and not simply in a one-sided relationship in which you expect everything from the other person and do not reciprocate to them. An important aspect of showing that you want to be equal Partners is using empathy.

This is more difficult than it sounds because we are all self-serving creatures. However, if you can show your partner that you do care about them outside of how it benefits you, that will go a long way in communicating to them your cared commitment. To show that you view both of you as equals and there needs and desires are as important as your own, you have to use empathy.

By stopping to listen to them, both the words they are saying, as well as the nonverbal communication they are using, you are showing them that they are important and that you want to have an understanding of how they feel. Everyone wants to feel as if their partner understands them, and truly here's what they are saying and what they mean.

Disagreements

Any healthy relationship is going to come into conflict or have a disagreement at some point in time, so you must know how to deal with this without it becoming overblown. Two people are invariably going to have different views on a situation, and this can be a great opportunity to learn about each other and grow together rather than become the ending point or a difficult situation in the relationship.

By using your emotional intelligence, you can't emphasize where your partner's coming from. Recognize both in yourself and them if this is a triggering situation that is going to cause a large emotional response and act accordingly. This might mean taking some time before discussing the situation, or it might mean simply recognizing and addressing that this has become a difficult topic, so both Partners can proceed gently.

It also requires a level of impulse control if you are feeling overwhelmed. By taking the space to hear out your partner rather than taking it as an attack to which you feel you have to reciprocate, you can self-regulate your emotions to grow from the situation.

Vulnerability

Because not all of us necessarily grew up with the best emotional role models in our lives, a lot of us have difficulties being vulnerable because we view them as weaknesses. It is a natural human instinct to protect our weaknesses to survive. The problem, however, is that emotional vulnerability is not something that is going to kill us, despite what are Primal instincts tell us.

To overcome this difficult obstacle and be vulnerable with our partner, we are communicating to them that we are being our fully authentic selves, and we trust them with our most difficult emotions. This is important to developing deep and personal relationships because, without a more intense level of self-disclosure, the relationship cannot be considered very close. This is something that should be reciprocated by both partners to show that they are on the same page about how intimate their relationship is, emotionally.

Honesty

An important aspect of having a healthy relationship is the ability to be honest with one another. Contrary to what many facetious people believe, this does not mean that you should say every mean thought that crosses your mind, but rather that you can be truthful in a respectful way at all times.

When people have a passing relationship or are simply friends or acquaintances, there can be a lot of tiptoeing around the truth to prevent any hurt feelings or misunderstandings.

When developing more personal relationships, it's is important that there is a level of trust that your partner does not want to hurt your feelings and acts accordingly. That means that when something comes up that they no might upset you, they do their best to communicate that to you in a gentle way.

That also means avoiding other unhealthy communication techniques such as not addressing the situation or using backhanded comments to beat around the bush. These are indicators that there is not a level of trust around emotions and being open to hearing difficult things.

Apologies

Perhaps the most difficult part of utilizing your emotional intelligence is admitting when you are wrong. However, this is a crucial step to ensuring your maturity and proving that you are using your skills. That being said, as you grow more practiced in all of your components of emotional intelligence, you will find it easier to admit when you are wrong and apologize.

This is a matter of understanding that your ego is not more important than the relationship itself. It is very common for a lot of us to want to be right about everything, but if that is taking the place of the emotions and well-being of your partner, then you need to start back at square one with learning emotional intelligence.

Part of coming to terms with being wrong and apologizing has to do with the impulse control that usually kicks in when your brain realizes you're wrong. Because your ego wants to protect itself, your brain goes into overdrive, coming up with excuses and blaming everything else that it can think of besides yourself. This is an opportunity for you to use your self-awareness to recognize this is a pattern and what you are feeling both physically and emotionally at that moment. It might take a lot of practice, but it is absolutely something that you can improve upon.

The great thing about being better at admitting you are wrong and apologizing is that you will not miss the sense of rightness you think you will be giving up. In fact, emotional intelligence helps you realize that it is not very important at all because you can better prioritize and contextualize the issue at hand. Rather than feeling a sense of resentment because you will apologize for things, you will actually feel a sense of freedom because you won't put as much importance on those things.

Chapter 8
Are Women More Emotionally Intelligent Than Men?

Empathy

This word comes up frequently when discussing emotional intelligence, as you may have noticed, considering it has been many a sub Point throughout this book so far. Many people consider empathy to be the master key to understanding emotional intelligence completely.

Scientifically, when it comes to empathy, this is taking place in a specific part of our brain, which collects information from our entire body. When we use empathy, it is literally our mind trying to copy how the other person is feeling. The specific part of our brain uses our entire body to recognize and help inform our own mind as to what the other person is feeling.

It just so happens that women keep the information they have acquired during the empathy process for how much longer amount of time than men do. This helps them to truly stay with the emotions of another person and feel the same desires to resolve the issue if it is a negative feeling, or celebrate and encouraged if it is a positive feeling.

On the flip side, a man's brain is less likely to hold on to those emotions, and instead, they will turn the switch to off and begin using a different part of their brain. This prevents memory from forming the emotional state both that the other person is in as well as preventing them from forming a memory of it in themselves. For this reason, they are less likely to be informed by emotion.

Negotiations

Of course, there is plenty we can utilize in our increased emotional intelligence to help us succeed in negotiations. The first thing we have to practice is an intense level of self-awareness and labeling our emotions. When we are in high-pressure situations such as negotiations, we are most likely going to have some intense emotions come up.

However, it is going to behoove us to keep those emotions under wraps to keep our Leverage. This is going to require an advanced level of self-regulation.

While appropriately expressing your emotions is something that you should do, in this situation, you do not want to express a lot of your emotions. A good way to do this is by mentally naming the emotion we are feeling to keep that emotion under control. By simply acknowledging it, you are going to take away a lot of its power.

Once you have done that, you can practice empathy to better understand how to maneuver in the negotiation. Rather than taking their offer at face value, you can attempt to decode the meaning behind what they are saying to find new footholds. By being more receptive to the nonverbal and verbal communication that the other party is putting out there, you will be more successful in understanding their emotions.

And perhaps most importantly, simply using your social skills to come across as a respectful, likable, appropriate communicator is something that cannot be understated.
Negotiations are a two-way conversation and will be much more enjoyable if it is done pleasantly. In fact, rather than thinking of negotiations as a win or lose situation, in reality, they are a win-win situation for both parties. If you can reframe the conversation in that manner and use your emotional intelligence to communicate that to the other party, everyone will walk away in better spirits.

Who Are the Better Leaders?

Of course, your sex or gender cannot determine if you will make a better leader or not, but everyone can learn from the other gender. The skills of being a great leader are accessible to everyone, but perhaps each individual has different elements to overcome to achieve emotional intelligence.

When it comes to showing that you are emotionally intelligent, women have an upper hand because it is expected that they are more emotional and therefore are more practiced in it.

This may or may not be true, but women and girls do get educated in this at a younger age more socially, on average in the United States. Men, on the other hand, might have felt that they were not supposed to become emotionally intelligent, and therefore have to seek it out on their own or overcome some conditioning that dissuaded them from learning about emotions.

It is too sweeping of a generalization to assert that one particular skill will make either men or women the better leader, but it is proven that the ability to learn and improve one's emotional intelligence is the same kind of initiative and openness that it takes to become a better leader.

Anyone open to collaborating and improving on their weak spots, as is required in acquiring emotional intelligence, is someone who has the determination and fortitude to seek out leadership positions.

Whether this means overcoming obstacles that are put in your way in advancing up the professional ladder, or overcoming social barriers that hindered your emotional growth prior to becoming an adult, if you are able to navigate the relationships to thrive in spite of these difficulties, you have been putting your emotional intelligence to work for you in showing that you are good leadership material.

Chapter 9
Empowering Your Social Skills

Mastering Basic Social Skills

Increasing your emotional intelligence is going to have an astounding impact on your entire life, most especially on an aspect of life that most people now are letting it drop by the wayside. Because of Technology's influence on how we live our day-to-day lives, the opportunity and ability to have face-to-face conversations is dwindling drastically. That means that if you can successfully navigate and have productive conversations, not only will you be light years ahead of others, but you will be able to pass on an invaluable life skill to others.

While it is not necessarily going to be something that feels totally comfortable to everyone all of the time, being able to have a conversation successfully will definitely become easier with practice as well as with the increase of your emotional intelligence. You will find that there are 4 steps to have a good conversation, all of which are components of emotional intelligence.

Not unlike the awareness necessary to notice your own emotions, the first part of having a great conversation is simply being aware of the other person. Obviously, this means notice that they are there, but it also means to notice and be aware of what exactly they are talking about, how they are communicating it, how they are feeling, how they are acting physically, and what you think they are trying to get out of this interaction. That does not mean everyone is just trying to use you to get something, but rather that some interactions have an explicit purpose, such as to assign a task at work, but others might simply be to have a pleasant interaction.

Be an Expert on Yourself

The absolute best thing about putting yourself out there in communication and social interactions is that you already are the expert on yourself. When other people are getting to know you, all they want to do is hear your expertise. There is no right or wrong answer, as long as you are not lying, because your thoughts, opinions, and views are unique to you and important to share with others to develop a relationship.

If you can build the confidence to have a conversation face-to-face with another person, you can build the confidence to show your most authentic self. Interestingly, we build confidence by practicing and succeeding. When it comes to social skills, you have been practicing your entire life. This conversation is just an extension of something you have already been doing successfully for many years.

On top of that, the fact that you are reading this book gives you an advantage over most people. Your interest and initiative in seeking out more education and learning how to practice these skills means you have everything it takes to succeed in casual conversation.

Simply reading this book should be a cause for celebration. You are spending more time on becoming an expert on yourself by learning ways to improve.

The Power of Verbal Communication

Much like the film industry, in the beginning, there were silent films, and of course, they were extremely popular. It was a masterful art form that people loved. However, once the ability to add sound to a film was invented, it broke the industry-wide open. Similarly, you can communicate non-verbally or through technology, and that may certainly get the job done and seem sufficient. You will find, though, that to communicate verbally, face-to-face will be drastically different and more powerful.

One massive disadvantage that communicating through technology rather than face to face has is the lack of inflection and emotion. Most information that we pick up when talking with another person comes through non-verbal communication, which includes how the words are said. That means that if you are texting or emailing someone, all of that emotion is lost.

To communicate verbally with another person contains exponentially more helpful information and helps to clarify much more quickly than other ways of communicating.

Beyond that, it allows you to practice the skills we are discussing in this book, which are drastically underutilized today. Because you are talking in real-time, you have to learn the art of being concise, because unlike an email you can take your time on, you are in a very real-time crunch because the other person's attention is a finite resource. Additionally, you will have to learn the art of give and take to have an effective conversation and keep your partner engaged.

Developing Good Listening Skills

For all of the advantages are modern technology offers in speed, connection, and keeping archives, one thing it cannot do is improve your listening skills. Reading off of your phone or computer, another person's message does not activate the muscles and skills necessary to be a good listener. So, learning how to become a good listener is a skill that will set you apart from most others.

Because in-person interactions are not achievable and retrievable like an email chain, oh, you have to be present and actively engaged at the moment to best retain what occurred. Not only does this help you to better remember this information, but it also makes the person you are communicating with feel valued and more likely to want to communicate with you again in the future.

Hearing Is Not Listening

Although they may seem identical, the difference between hearing and listening is vast. To be able to hear is simply a physical function of noticing that sounds are being made. Listening, however, is the active pursuit of paying attention to what is being communicated. Knowing and applying the differences will make all the difference in the world.

To actively show that you are listening, you will use verbal and nonverbal Clues to indicate your engagement. You will also need to clarify or ask questions that show you understand and want more information about what the other person is saying. This tells them that they are important to you, and what they are saying is valuable. It also indicates that they are being truly understood, which is what everyone wants on a primal level.

What Is the Purpose of Listening?

Listening is how you put your emotional intelligence components into action. Through the act of actively listening, you are becoming more self-aware because you are practicing this by recognizing your own emotions that are occurring in response to what they are saying. You are self-regulating for the same reason. You are emphasizing with what the other person is saying, especially if you are truly actively engaged. You are improving your social skills, no matter how poorly you think you are doing at the conversation. Finally, you are exercising your motivation and learning more about how to find deeper wells of your internal motivation to continue this conversation or inspire more.

Some other reasons it's important to listen is to simply create Connections in the world. As discussed earlier, we require human connection, so listening can help us have an easier time in doing so.

It also helps you humble yourself to put yourself, your concerns, and other issues into perspective. If you live a life entirely inside of your mind, you will have no point of view that allows then outside perspectives, contacts, or values. This helps you learn critical thinking skills to better adjust your thoughts and opinions.

Obstacles to Listening Skills

In today's world, it seems like everything is actually trying to actively prevent people from having good listening skills. Every aspect of most of our technological advances separates us from the need for good listening skills. By making everything automated, eliminating human interactions, and creating addictive apps and computer programs, we are becoming less able to practice or even tolerate the kind of patients and failure it takes to be good listeners.

Perhaps the most difficult part of good listening skills is keeping eye contact. Rather than being distracted by your phone or other screens, if you can keep your eyes focused on the person you are communicating with, they will feel you are truly understanding and hearing them, which will make them trust you more.

This and many other nonverbal communication techniques will be discussed at length in the next chapter.

Practice Empathy

Another unfortunate side effect of our technological advances is that by eliminating the human element and face-to-face interaction, our brains get less opportunity and practice and using empathy. In fact, that region of our brain does not get activated nearly as often as it used to. It is not a coincidence that online bullying is an epidemic. Between the lack of connection between the bully and the victim, both physically and visually, as well as the anonymity available to the bully, separating them from the results of their harsh Behavior, there is little opportunity for empathy to occur there.

This is not easy, but it is very important in your development of both emotional intelligence and, honestly, creating a better world for everyone who exists in it. Some ways to practice empathy include taking some time when you are feeling emotional before responding.

This can me neither using meditation to find a sense of peace nor even just counting to ten before reacting. Both of these will help you create space between the overwhelming impulse you have to respond emotionally rather than logically and empathetically. By taking time, you can better consider all of your options as well as the outcomes of those options for acting drastically.

Chapter 10
Boost Your Social EQ with These Powerful Verbal and Nonverbal Clues

It is crucially important to keep in mind that all verbal and nonverbal clues are based entirely on the culture, and for our purposes, we are discussing those of the US. In fact, many of the things we discuss here are the complete opposite in other parts of the world.

Body Language

Our bodies can tell other people a lot about what we are thinking and feeling without even using words. Posture, for instance, is one of the first things another person might notice about you.

How you are holding yourself, whether that is slouched, leaning, or ramrod straight. All of these things communicate different meanings, two other people.

Appearing hunched over or slumped down tells other people you are bored, tired, disinterested, or even lacking confidence. By trying to make yourself smaller, shorter, or less noticeable, you are communicating a level of timidness or a desire for distance. By appearing tall, straight spine, with your chin up, and your chest open, you are communicating the opposite. You will come across as feeling confident in yourself, interested in those around you, and happy to be there.

Arms and legs

Much like our posture, the positioning of our arms and legs can also tell other people a lot about our current emotions. If someone's using their arms or legs to cross in front of themselves, this can often mean they are trying to put up a barrier, both physically and emotionally, with the person they are talking to. By closing themselves and separating from those around them, they might be disinterested, overwhelmed, intimidated, or even hostile.

On the flip side, if you want to make sure you are communicating that you are open, interested, engaged, and friendly, you should do your best not to put up physical barriers between you and the person you're the indicated with.

Hands and feet

By being fidgety or constantly moving our hands, we communicate a sense of being rushed or busy. Especially if you are tapping your fingers or have something in your hand that you are tapping rapidly, this sends the message that you have somewhere else you would rather be, or perhaps that you are nervous. Of course, similarly to the above-mentioned body language, if you use your hands to cover your face or create a barrier, that will come across as disinterested.

Your feet are also a kind of secret communicator. When you are interested in who you are speaking with or what you are talking about, your feet will most likely point in their direction. If, however, you are not interested, you will most likely unconsciously turn your feet away from them to subconsciously communicate that you would like to get away.

Distance

Most people have a natural range of what they consider personal space, which means that unless you have a close and personal relationship with someone, almost everyone wants you to stay at least two to four feet away from them.

Of course, by invading that personal space, you are communicating a few things, depending on the situation. If you are also giving off other intimate types of nonverbal cues, you might be trying to tell them that you are interested in becoming more intimate with them. You could also combine the invasion with more aggressive types of nonverbal cues, and that would communicate that you are trying to be dominant and powerful over them.

On the flip side, when you stand too far away from someone when you are trying to communicate, that tells them that you are trying to be emotionally distant as well as physically.

Facial Expressions

There are six universal and overarching facial expressions that we all share: surprise, happiness, sadness, fear, anger, and disgust. These all use our entire faces, incorporating the muscles around our eyes, eyebrows, mouth, and jaw, and sometimes our nose.

These are also nonverbal clues that we give off unconsciously, whether we want to or not. Sometimes they are big responses, but if you want to hide your emotions and you try to prevent these actions from happening, they will still occur, and it is called a micro expression.

Eyes

Eye contact can tell us so much. If you have ever felt bored in a conversation and thought you could slyly look away, to your phone, to a clock, or another person, it is almost guaranteed you were not sly at all, and that person got the message that you were not interested in what they have to say. Conversely, if you spend too much time staring at someone, especially if you are not even in a conversation with them, then you probably make them feel uncomfortable.

When communicating a respectful amount of interest, it is commonly understood that it is best to form a type of triangle of eye contact, moving between looking into one of the other person's eyes for a few seconds, and looking at the other, before looking to their mouth for a few seconds. This shows that you are engaged but not showing signs of aggression.

Mouth

The most common way we usually think of our mouth is if we are smiling with happiness or frowning in sadness. Actually, there are a few other ways we use our mouth for nonverbal clues, as well.

When we cover our mouths, that often indicates that we are trying to hide something, not unlike when we put up a barrier by crossing our arms, but because this is associated with the words we are saying, this makes people think you are lying. Perhaps try bringing your finger to your chin to communicate thought without the negative connotation of deception.

When we are seen biting our lips or chewing the side of our cheeks, this tells others that we are nervous, confused, and not confident. To show a healthy kind of consideration, try pursing your lips instead. Make sure it is not too long or too stern, as you do not want to come across as strict.

Head movement

It is very common to see someone nod in agreement and shake their head in disagreement. However, did you know you most likely do this unconsciously as well? This is another example of a microexpression that is very difficult to prevent yourself from doing, which leaks out your true emotions, whether you want them to come out or not.

To communicate engagement and interest, it is also good to tilt your head to the side slightly--we often associate this with a dog listening to its owner. Often, we also tend to raise our head when we become more interested in what we are hearing and lower it down if we are feeling somehow defensive about what we are hearing.

Mirroring

When we want to communicate that we are on the same page as another person, we can use mirroring techniques to show that we are similar. By matching their height, --if possible-- body position, volume, pace, and movements, we are showing that we are in sync. Often, though, this is something that happens unconsciously when two people truly are in sync. However, you can do it consciously to put others at ease or show your interest.

Tone of voice

This is a combination of a few things, all of which come together to indicate emotion. The inflection you use, the emphasis throughout, and if your nonverbal actions match the words you are saying all play into your tone of voice. For example, sarcasm is simply when your words are opposite to your tone of voice. This will make you come across as untrustworthy or even rude. Similarly, inflection is merely emphasizing different parts of your words, which can drastically change the meaning. By using inflection properly, you will seem thoughtful. Without it, you will come across as monotone and dull.

Speed of speech

To merely be understood, how quickly you speak is important. If your rate is too high, people will not be able to keep up with what you are saying, and they might think you are nervous or have somewhere else to be. Speaking too slowly, however, will communicate that maybe you are distracted, confused, or even bored.

It is also important to change up the speed of your speaking throughout your conversations to help indicate that you are engaged, are emphasizing certain things, or trying to keep others interested.

In today's fast-paced world, it might take some conscious effort to slow down your speech if you are used to communicating via technology, which happens almost instantaneously. Conversely, if you are quite out of practice communicating verbally, you may need to practice expressing your thoughts more quickly.

Verbal clues

Other things such as volume are also important. For instance, if you are too quiet, people will often take that as a sign of being timid or lacking confidence. Being too loud, however, indicates arrogance and being inconsiderate. It also depends on your location and the context of what the appropriate volume should be.

Similarly, enunciating is important to be understood, so mumbling your words comes across as being unsure of yourself or meek. Over enunciating, however, can be seen as an indicator that you are being condescending.

There is also the quality of vocality, such as how raspy or breathy the words come out. This is often a sign of sensuality, so it is not appropriate for work relationships.

Environmental clues

Today we are always carrying our phones in our hand or pocket, which causes its host of nonverbal problems. Whenever we turn our attention away from the person, we are communicating in person with to instead focus on our phone, we are telling them that they are less important to us than our phone.

This makes them less likely to feel warmly toward you, which in turn makes them less likely to either continue or initiate further communication with you. Much like our phones, any outside environmental stimuli that draws your attention away from them will cause this same effect. If possible, it is courteous to apologize for the distraction and re-engage to show you are still interested.

As discussed earlier, using your own body as a barrier between yourself and others communicates an attempt to distance yourself from them. That can also be done using actual physical objects. If someone is holding something between the two of you, especially if it is close to their person and especially over their chest, they are most likely trying to prevent either the entire conversation or simply certain information from getting out. However, this can also be done with furniture, such as chairs, desks, or tables. In this case, they are trying to communicate the amount of personal space they desire, which you should respect.

Chapter 11
Transforming Emotions into Emotional Intelligence

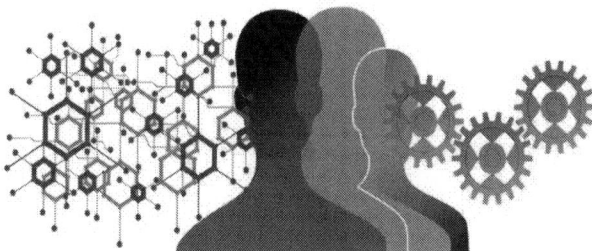

Emotions are Valuable

Our emotions are very valuable in living our life, creating our thoughts, and predicting how we behave. In fact, absolutely everything we do, every move we make, every thought we have is due to an emotion. Whether they are fleeting emotions or are deep-seated feelings, they are important to feel and to understand.

A major outcome of having emotions is the actions we take because of them. If you understand that you are repeatedly making the same bad decision over and over because of a desire to either feel an emotion or overcome an emotion you no longer want to feel, only then can you truly deal with the best way to break that pattern.

You will be more successful in avoiding the triggers, as well as overcoming it entirely once you understand its roots.

This also is true for our Primal instincts for survival. That is why d notification sounds we get on our phones increase the stress in our brain and body. It is an alarm sound, which tells our lizard brain that there is danger. Of course, we know that is not true, but our body feels the emotions associated with a danger to our lives. So as effective as it is at getting us to respond quickly by answering our phones, it also creates other actions and emotions in ourselves.

Manage Your Negative Emotions

Depending on your preferences, personality type, and the situation, there are many ways you can attempt to manage your negative emotions. Perhaps the best way is to take a deep dive into trying to understand them. Not only will this require empathy and a healthy dose of gentleness on yourself, but it will also require a lot of introspection and thought. If you understand some of the physiological reasons that emotions occur, this can help you understand your reactions to them. If you can pinpoint the source of an emotion, you can potentially eliminate the emotional response chew it in the future.

Another way to manage negative emotions, whether you truly understand where they stem from or not, is to change your actions or try to eliminate the triggering elements that make you feel them. You do not have to know why looking at social media makes you feel bad, all you have to do is minimize the amount of time you are on social media. Alternatively, if your lack of action is what creates the negative emotion, you can create positive reinforcement Loops that encourage you to take positive action.

Finally, you can also practice other acts that give you an appropriate outlet for letting off steam when you do have negative emotions. There are certainly some things that we all must do in our lives that are not pleasant, we do not enjoy, and truly bring up negativity. If you cannot alter it, and understanding the source of it does not help, you can create an opportunity to deal with pent-up physical, mental, and emotional stressors they bring. This can be by creating art, working out, doing yoga, enjoying nature, going to therapy, or anything else that helps healthily.

Convert Emotions into Emotional Intelligence

When you can truly think about and understand emotions, whether they are positive or negative, you will be better equipped to convert them into emotional intelligence. This is because you will begin to normalize the practice of recognizing, managing, and intellectualizing emotions altogether. Absolutely everyone has them and they can teach you something.

Even the emotions that we think of as negative truly are meant to inform us of some part of our brain that needs assistance. They are a type of alarm that tells us how close to or far away from health and happiness we are. As already discussed, they are the impetus for taking action, which is the basis of our entire lives. They also allow you to get closer to understanding your authentic self and presenting it to the world.

What Is Motivation?

Truly, motivation comes from every single part of your life, from your mental, physical, spiritual, emotional, and social aspects of your being. This means there are not only a million different reasons why you don't do something, but it also means there are a million different ways to approach doing something. When it comes to truly successfully motivating yourself, it requires that you have a reason why you want to do it.

Something has to activate inside of you to take action. Next, you must persist through the obstacles that you are trying to overcome. Finally, you must have a level of intensity that outputs enough effort to achieve the action. Each situation is different and requires different levels of all three of these things, but all three elements must be present to create motivation.

The Motivation to Change

There are potentially three different things that inspire us to change. Any combination of the three can be at work at any given time.

Some of our motivation comes from our animal instincts. These are Primal urges we have to survive, thrive, and protect ourselves. Biologically, our body reacts to these things being threatened, so sometimes the motivation that comes from our instincts don't even pass through most of our brain, rather they are knee-jerk reactions that our body makes without even thinking about it.

The next level of motivation also is associated with Primal desires, but are less pressing. These are drives and needs that we have, but they are more in our control. For instance, you may be hungry, but you also have the self-control to wait until dinner rather than immediately running out of the room to find food.

Lastly, our bodies and Minds have preferred levels of arousal. This means that if you are bored, you are not filling the preferred level. Alternatively, if you are overwhelmed or scared, you have become too aroused.

Achieve Your Goals

The best way to achieve your goals is to harness the knowledge you have about motivation and make it work for you. To fight against it is to ignore science and make things more difficult for yourself.

The first thing you want to do is write your goal down. Put pen to paper, and make it official in the universe and outside of your head. That way, you can refer to it as often as needed. Next, you will want to break your goal down into different measurements. How specific can you get in enumerating your goal? What is the time frame you want to achieve it in? How can you measure its success? These are all necessary questions to answer in order to succeed.

Finally, now that you have all the information you need, make a detailed step-by-step plan from where you are now until it is completed. Do not leave out any minute step. Part of going through your list of two dues is going to be celebrating every single element as you cross it off your list.

Practical Tips for Finding Motivation

A simple way to help you find your motivation is to be in a good mood. Rather than viewing an obstacle as something negative you have to overcome, if you can recognize it as the learning opportunity that it is and see it as a chance for you to prove yourself, you will have more success in attempting it.

As just mentioned, celebrating every tiny Victory along the way serves as continued and ongoing motivation throughout your journey. This isn't merely a perfunctory pat on the back, but it is truly recognizing that every large goal is achieved One Step at a Time.

If you know that living up to other people's expectations is a big motivating factor in your life, then find support in another person. Whether that means telling someone else what your goal is, asking a friend to check in on you to keep you on track, or even joining a support group whose explicit purpose is to help motivate all participants toward a similar goal, you can make your understanding of your own emotions work for you.

Similar to our impulse control, understanding the long-term goal for why we are striving for something can help reignite our motivation. Knowing the reason, you are making a short-term sacrifice can help ease the blow if you have an important vision in the future.

Lastly, tell yourself you are only going to get started and do it for 30 seconds. Oftentimes, the most difficult part of going toward a goal is getting started. To overcome the stagnation of not taking an action, promise yourself that you will only begin and keep going for 30 seconds. After that, you can stop if you want, but most likely you will want to continue. It is easier to keep going then it is to stop again.

Chapter 12

Practical Steps to Improve Your Emotional Intelligence Skills

Step 1: Observing How You Feel

This is something that is going to take practice but it is crucial to improving your emotional intelligence. It requires that you use it in real-time. You cannot practice it theoretically, this is something that has to be done practically in a real-life Laboratory. Whenever you are feeling an emotion that is strong enough to notice yet not so overwhelming that you have difficulty with your impulse control around it, that is a perfect time to begin trying to name or label the emotion you are having.

Take some time to pause and spend a few moments in this introspective space. This can be done silently in your mind, out loud, or even written down in a journal. Acknowledge the emotion you are feeling. Call it what it is. Recognize how it is manifesting itself in your body. Imagine it is an entity that is standing outside of your body, as if a statue that you can look at it. Understand that while it is something that you felt inside of you, it is also something that can leave your body and mind. It is not a part of you.

Step 2: Paying Attention to How You Behave

Now it's time to take note of your physical behaviors. Were you doing something was a direct response or reaction to that emotion? Did you take action without even thinking about it? Did you have an Impulse that you find difficult to control? These are all important questions to ask if you have especially overwhelming emotions.

This is not restricted to only those intense emotions, though. Perhaps you simply have a pattern of behavior that you were not even aware of.

These could be simple and triggered by even small emotions. Indeed, you cannot control the emotions you have, rather the only thing you can control is your behavior around it.

Most likely, your behaviors and actions you take as a response or reaction to an emotion is to satisfy some sort of need. So, in this process, you may recognize you take some behaviors that are not healthy or that you would like to change. This is the moment where you try to understand why you behave that way.

Step 3: Managing Your Negative Emotions

As discussed earlier, there are many ways to approach managing your negative emotions. The simplest way is to stop taking actions that make you feel bad or create negative emotions. Of course, this is easier said than done. However, sometimes it truly is as simple as that. Oftentimes, we are more in control of our situations than we give ourselves credit for, which creates negative emotions and a sense of unease, which triggers bad coping mechanisms.

Much like the children in the marshmallow study, a very effective way to manage your negative emotions is to distract yourself from them. Do not allow yourself to get caught up in either worrying about the future or ruminating about the past, because neither of those things are in your control or applicable to the present moment.

Not unlike our technique to inspire motivation, tell yourself you are going to pretend to feel another way for just 30 seconds. You can even fake a smile or think about something that makes you laugh for just a few moments, and oftentimes this will truly counteract the negative emotion. By getting your mind onto something else as well as taking a physical action associated with a more positive emotion, you can trick your mind into momentarily going along.

Step 4: Practicing Empathizing with Yourself and Others

You must be gentle with yourself during this process because it is a learning and growing process. It is also important to note, that this process is ongoing and lasts the rest of your life. That's one way to say you have to be gentle to yourself for the rest of your life! Being able to practice empathy with yourself is important to continue growing. You are going to fail sometimes and have difficult situations that you didn't respond to in the absolute best way. That is all right. That is part of the process.

One way to practice empathy with yourself is to think of yourself as you would one of your friends. Oftentimes we are much harder on ourselves and we speak and think very harshly concerning our thoughts and actions. When in reality, if a friend of ours did, said, or thought the same thing, we would never be so cruel to them. You need to become your friend to be gentle with yourself.

You can also practice empathy with yourself and others by recognizing all of us for exactly what we are: mere humans. As discussed throughout this book, we are just a collection of organs, skin, and bones all clumped together trying to navigate the impulses and stimuli coming into our brain. For that reason, we are all doing pretty well to simply be reading this book and trying to apply its principles. When you can think of people as Primal animals who are just doing their best to be civilized and utilize the massive brain we have been given, it is much easier to have compassion for and forgive when we do something sort of dumb.

Step 5: Using a Positive Style of Communication

When you go into interactions with that kind of mindset, it is much easier to use a positive style of communication. If you consider the amount of concern, anxiety, or worries you have, it's easy to imagine that most of the people around you have those very same considerations. For that reason, we can go into every interaction with a level of equanimity and understanding which allows for a more positive experience.

Other people can sense when you are being positive, kind, compassionate, and understanding. They can also feel the opposite, so by merely having the right mindset and intention from the outset, you can often set the tone for the rest of the conversation simply with your mind. Additionally, you can continue to communicate positive intentions throughout based on your nonverbal communication as discussed in chapter 10.

Step 6: Creating a Positive Environment and Bouncing Back from Adversity

To best facilitate continued, ongoing, and expected positive communication, you have to create an environment routinely that can be considered positive. This means it will need to become a practice and a pattern for it to become an expectation. While it is not especially difficult, it does take quite a bit of consideration. Of course, you must continue to use empathy in your interactions, but also approaching it with a positive mindset that facilitates an all-around winning situation for simply communicating is crucial. It is also important that you bring your authentic self to the interaction to show that you are a person with emotions and you are putting the relationship above the outcome.

When you can create that positive environment, it becomes a habit and a recurring event that you can depend upon. This will serve you well when dealing with adversity. Bay help create the foundation that will allow you to bounce back. You may not have "gotten it right" in every moment, but just like your positive environment, you have "gotten it right" in the past and you can again. It also sets the stage for you to be able to talk to your supportive friends about this difficult situation for you.

Step 7: Desiring to Help Others Succeed (And Succeed Yourself)

When you work on your emotional intelligence, you will find that your empathy translates into a truly deep and meaningful desire for others to succeed. While this may seem martyr-like or completely unselfish, it is more a result of the fact that you understand that's life truly is not a competition. Everyone can succeed, and the more often others around you succeed, the better you and everyone feels.

Because you are a human, and as we have already established, humans need connection and interaction, it only makes sense that you will feel better if the people around you feel better. And because emotional intelligence components expound upon each other, The More You Learn and Grow, healthier you will become, which will affect the people around you.

Your desires are not completely self-serving, because they grow healthier the higher your emotional intelligence grows. It is not a technique to merely manipulate others for your gain, rather you begin to realize the process and outcome is its reward.

Step 8: Emotional Intelligence as a Lifetime Process (Being Motivated)

As you may have noticed, there is no end goal or high score for emotional intelligence. Rather, it is an act of continued learning, growing, and education. That means it is a journey rather than a destination. All of these components we begin learning from birth, and ideally, we will continue to learn until the end of our lives.

Some ways to ensure we continue feeling motivated shows increase our emotional intelligence is to recognize it for exactly what it is. This means that rather than celebrating a specific achievement, we should celebrate the process we took to get there. We don't have to have a "perfect conversation," rather it is important that we tried and practiced.

Surrounding yourself with people who are also empathetic, have compassion, and are open to learning and increasing their emotional intelligence can also serve as great motivation to keep you a lifelong student. If you are constantly belittled or having to explain that you are trying your best, that can take its toll on you. Instead, if you can find supportive friends who are willing to admit they are fallible and are trying to improve themselves as well, you are more likely to be inspired to continue.

Chapter 13
Leadership

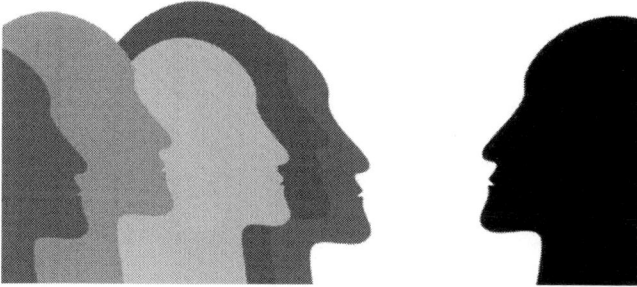

Definition

Very simply, a leader is the person in charge. This can take many forms and shapes, and often isn't enumerated. For our purposes, however, we want something more than this. It is an important role that sets the stage for your team and the task at hand. As a leader, you provide inspiration and direction, motivation, and support, as well as having the path to success. For a good leader, the end goal is not the only thing you keep in mind. You are considerate of your employees, their motivations, their communication styles, and how they contribute to the team.

Of course, we have all had bosses and leaders throughout our lives, but being in charge does not bestow you with the skills of that of a good leader. To be a great leader, you must have some skills and practice your emotional intelligence. Thankfully, these are all things you can acquire and get better at over time. Even if you do not have a role that is explicitly managing others, you can still be a leader in your peer group. If you act respectfully, continue to actively show that you have emotional intelligence, you can be relied upon, you are helpful, and you act per the rules of your hierarchy, you most certainly can still be considered a leader in practice, if not its name.

The Leadership Maturity Continuum Model by Stephen R. Covey

From his world-famous book *"The 7 Habits of Highly Effective People"*, Stephen Covey Posited that to truly be a great leader you had to have a high level of maturity, which shows up on a continuum with three levels that we transition and growth through as we become more educated and older.

This is a growth that only happens mentally and emotionally, rather than physically. Unfortunately, not all of us will grow through all of the levels, because it does take a conscious effort to learn the lessons required to become emotionally mature as a leader.

Dependency

As children, we are dependent upon others for everything. This is the lowest level of maturity. We cannot take care of ourselves in any way, shape, or form as small children, so our development begins with needing others to survive. This is when our attention is entirely focused on others taking care of us. As we gain more control over our bodies and our brains begin to develop, we slowly but surely learn some tasks to begin taking care of ourselves.

Independence

We consider adulthood to be when we learn how to live independently of others. Rather than being taken care of, we take care of ourselves. This is a sign of maturity, which is why it is the second level in his continuum. Your attention is still mostly focused on yourself, but because you are autonomous, rather than focusing on others satisfying your needs, you are more internally focused.

Interdependence

This is the highest level of maturity in which a person recognizes that when people work together, more, and better things can be accomplished. So rather than focusing on what others can do for you and rather than focusing on how you can accomplish something alone, this is when you realize that everyone relies on everyone.

Styles of Leadership

There is not a consensus on how many different types of leadership there are. Some people say three up to 12 different our purposes we will discuss that there are five general different types of leadership styles. No one leadership style is inherently better or worse than the other but they all have different qualities and come naturally to different types of people. The most important thing to remember about leadership styles is that they all have an important role just not necessarily in every situation. What is the perfect leadership style for one situation could spell disastrous results for another. Here are five different types of leadership styles will be discussing today.

Delegate

A leader who delegates does not participate along with the people they are leading. They direct and lead from above. They could likely stand at a podium and not interact with the people they oversee. They are a very hands-off type of leader. They do not focus on the individual or individuals they are leading; they only focus on the end goal and if the things are happening to get the team to that finish line.

This type of leader does not do great at motivating. For an entrepreneur or someone who works freelance, this type of leadership style works best for them. There is an end goal and the team or employee works on their own using their internal motivation to complete the task at hand.

Transactional

A transactional leader is one who in most instances is something like the stereotypical boss caricature. They provide payment for services completed. The main motivating factor for these types of leaders is being able to provide something for the team, most frequently that thing is money. These leaders know that the motivating factor is external.

They do not focus on the individual, their goals, or their internal motivation. Oftentimes this is a style seen most commonly in minimum wage type jobs. There is a reward and punishment system setup that delineates it so the team knows ahead of time what the outcome will be based on their actions. The internal motivation is not a big factor in this type of leadership style, however, there are a lot of "best practices" already set up to ensure a predictable outcome if the team members follow them.

This type of leadership style is seen in a lot of workplaces and works great for those purposes. This type of leadership style would not be successful necessarily in a setting such as a preschool. For example, this type of leadership in that setting would be seen as cold and heartless in that setting.

Autocrat

The leader who is an autocrat likes to be in complete control. They do not participate with the people they are leading. Communication often only goes one way and that is from the leader downward. Autocratic leaders tend to be more micromanagers and nitpicky. They want to have complete control over the entire process and know exactly what everyone in the team is doing at all times. This type of leader feels they know everything that needs to be known about the end goal of the team, and therefore they are the all-knowing leader and director for that reason.

An autocratic leader is reminiscent of a drill sergeant. For some purposes, this is the perfect type of leadership for the team below them. For others, this is not satisfactory to most. For instance, a drill sergeant in the military is expected to have complete control over the privates they are superior to, and for that reason, it is a complimentary leadership style for everyone involved. For other teams, however, this style would not be a pleasant experience for most involved.

Democrat

This type of leadership is reminiscent of the type of politics we use in the United States of America. The democratic leader considers thoughts, opinions, and input of all of the people on their team, rather than just controlling everyone in it. They know that everyone on the team has something to contribute, and therefore everyone on the team is important. This type of leadership style can be seen in a lot of places, most notably the United States of America's voting process.

While this type of leadership style is effective at keeping all members of the team engaged, it is not a very quick method of problem-solving or task of signing. It does take time to hear everyone's input and transform all of the options laid on the table into one actionable solution.

Transformative

A transformative leader is the rarest of all leadership styles. This type of leader not only knows that the team has to be involved, but they also know that they are individuals working on the best way to achieve that goal. Transformative leaders use the internal motivation of the team members and provide external motivation that is in line with each individual. This type of leadership uses the best of both worlds to maximize the efficiency and effectiveness of the individuals of the team, as well as the team as a whole, to achieve the greater outcome they desire.

This type of leadership uses a little bit of all of the types of leadership in perfect balance. A transformative leader, however, does not get bogged down in micromanaging, but rather uses the charm and vision to motivate all team members to perform their best. This type of leader empowers the members to make some of their own choices while still navigating everyone down the same path to most effectively achieve the team's goal.

Chapter 14
Leader Competencies

Constructing a Vision

As a leader, you are tasked with getting a team to a specific goal. You are the Middle Point between success and the people who are on their way there. To truly be a good leader, you must have a vision that you can effectively communicate to your team which motivates them to keep the end goal in mind.

This is a collection of explicit statements and values, as well as a more vague culture and the actions of the team. All of these can and should be directed by the leader. The Energy of the team should be a reflection of the leader. If there is a disconnect in that, you can rest assured there will be a disconnect in the work of the team concerning the end call.

For most companies, their overall end goal feels very far-reaching and disconnected from the action's employees take every day. This is where a great leader steps in to make that connection for them. They help employees understand the importance of every menial task they do, even the unenjoyable one. It is true that it takes a village, and making sure your employees can see the bigger picture despite their micro Zoom point of view is crucial in helping them understand that the company wouldn't work without them.

Inspiration and Motivation

Of course, the promise of a paycheck inspires some people to some extent, but ideally, a great leader will provide more than that simple transactional one. Everyone wants to know that they are contributing. We all want to be helpful in our lives. This is especially true when you consider that work takes up approximately a third of our adult life. Understandably, your employees will want to feel that they are not only contributing positively to their work environment but that their work is contributing positively to the world.

Good leaders understand this about their employees and serve as inspiration and motivation in challenging times. By providing the story of their role within the company and the impact their work has on the company's success, this can help remind people of why they started working there in the first place. It also serves as inspiration to push through the more difficult or boring tasks that seemingly are not beneficial. This is also important in establishing the culture of your team by making sure it is a positive place that keeps perspective to maintain a sustainable effort.

Management of the Vision

For your vision to be successful, however, it must be a story and a vision that everyone on your team understands and is on board with. To achieve this, you need buy-in from everyone on the team. Everyone has their own individual goals in life. To get everyone to buy-in to your team's goal, however, is when everyone agrees that by achieving this goal, they will be helping themselves in some way? To have a team buy into the vision, the goal, or the result, is to have a team that will be dedicated to a process and completion.

A good leader will help the team see themselves as a crucial part of completing the task, as well as feeling ownership of their role and accountability for their actions. Whether it is a shared vision or a feeling of mastery, a good leader will know that the most effective mindset for a team is to get everyone to buy into it rather than feeling disconnected from it.

This requires an ongoing check-in process in which the leader talks with the team, both collectively and individually, to make sure that along the way everyone still feels but they have ownership over their work.

This is easy to achieve in the beginning, while adrenaline is pumping and the novelty of a new task makes it appealing. As time goes on, however, while the novelty wears off and your employees have run into different hardships, it becomes more difficult and that much more important for the leader to manage the vision.

Coaching and Teamwork

A good leader knows that a mountain may seem impossible to climb, but the only way to climb it is to put one foot in front of the other and just keep climbing. It may seem out of reach for a very long time, but there are no shortcuts, so the only way to accomplish the end goal is to persist in trying. Both for themselves and to remind their teammates that a persistent mindset will always outperform a defeatist mindset. A good leader knows that with any journey there will be difficulties and setbacks, so not to give up or let them give up at the first sign of stress.

Not only do they prepare their team to look out for these hard times, but a great leader tells them how to overcome those obstacles to continue along. One of the greatest assets of persistence is the feeling of accomplishment one gets after figuring out how to successfully overcome a challenge. So, it is the leader's job not only to see the challenge as an opportunity, but also to help their team learn from it, and it will become a strength going forward.

Leadership Skills

Every good leader needs to be optimistic about the goal and the team. This is a matter of victim mentality or an autonomous mentality. Good leaders know that they are fully in control of their team, their thoughts, and their actions, therefore they are optimistic that things will go well and they can correct things when they go astray. This is not just a matter of blind optimism, but instead, it is a deep knowledge that they truly are in full control of their situation.

A great way to keep optimism up both in yourself as a leader and among your team is to celebrate victories and communicate positive outcomes. Because some mountains seem too high to scale, it's important that every Peak and step climbed be recognized as the success that it is. This is especially true when working with a team. To recognize the individual contributions that people make to the overall goal. This lets everyone know that you truly are appreciative of them as individuals.

The Ideal Leader

One cannot measure the success of leadership without considering the performances that come from their team and whether or not they accomplish their goals. A great leader knows how to get the best output and the best performances from their team members. It is not enough to simply be liked by everyone or be positive about the outcome, but the result must match the optimism. The end goal is truly the measure of success at work, and it doesn't matter if you take every other box of being a good leader, if you cannot meet the goal, your leadership is lacking.

Part of this is the idea that the whole is greater than the sum of the parts. The output is greater as a team rather than as a bunch of individuals which is why you are here as the leader to make that happen. By being a good leader, you inspire the team to work better than they would on their own. This helps to eliminate feelings of competitiveness and critiquing, which provides more productive and efficient workplaces.

Chapter 15
Behavioral Communication

Behavior

Behavior is the way that we Act, the actions we take, whether alone or concerning others. This is rather all-encompassing, because not only do our movements and nonverbal communication count as Behavior but also are verbal communication is a behavior as well. This means that internal actions such as thoughts are not Behavior. However, our thoughts can turn into behaviors. If they are intentional behaviors, then these are conscious behaviors. There are also actions we take as a direct result of our thoughts that we do not even think about when they happen, and these are unconscious behaviors.

When it comes to our emotional intelligence and applying it to be a better leader, you must do a self-analysis and figure out what type of Behavioral Communicator you are as well as what type of Behavioral Communicator you want to be. I will give you a hint, there's only one that utilizes a high level of emotional intelligence, and therefore it is the only one that can truly be a great leader without causing harm to others. There is also only one that resides in the highest level of the leadership maturity Continuum as discussed in the previous chapter. Unsurprisingly, the one that requires the highest emotional intelligence as well as the highest emotional maturity are one and the same.

While it is not easy at all to change your behavioral communication Style for the better, it is absolutely worth the effort. It is going to require a lot of introspection and studying on your own, but it is perhaps one of the most effective ways to increase your emotional intelligence. It might require that you think back to your childhood and the lessons you learned about how to communicate, how emotions were dealt with, what was valued from you, and what you had to do to survive emotionally and possibly physically.

For these reasons, it is often best to attempt to understand the source and potentially change your behaviors with the help of a professional, such as a therapist.

Behavioral Communication

We already know that we communicate verbally using our words and non-verbally in a myriad of ways. However, there is another aspect of communication called behavioral communication. This is a combination of both verbal and nonverbal communication. It tends to be more of an unconscious Style that is based on how we learned to communicate, most often from our parents and family, how we learned to deal with emotions, again from childhood, and our various feelings in the moment when we are communicating.

Behavioral communication is a study of psychology which controls the different ways that we express our emotions, thoughts, and needs as an attempt to communicate with others. This happens mostly indirectly and non-verbally. This can be done directly or indirectly, consciously, or unconsciously, verbally, or non-verbally.

This is an especially nuanced study of psychology, which most people do not delve into, and requires an intense level of introspection to determine for yourself.

While each individual has one that tends to be most natural and used most often in our lives, we all can and do cycle through these depending on the situation. Oftentimes, the type of Behavioral communication evolved throughout our lifetime as our maturity and education improve, changing hour Personal Style. However, we can also alter our behavioral communication style, usually unconsciously, depending on individual moments. Certain contacts give us different roles and we have different understandings of how we should act depending upon those.

There are pros and cons to all four of the different types of Behavioral communication Styles, and some are more appropriate at certain times than others. There is no one right or wrong way to communicate, and in fact, most people will use all four both appropriately and inappropriately throughout their life.

Types of Behavioral Communication

Aggressive Behavioral Communication

Aggression is a type of hostility or violence perceived by either Behavior or attitude, which is often considered to be an attack or confrontation. So, when we are looking at aggressive behavioral communication, we understand these to be the actions of a person who is aggressive. while this can certainly takes a form of a fight or physical altercation, which is what we most often think of when we consider aggressive behavioral communication, it's doesn't have to be that explicit.

The way that aggressive communicators Act in their everyday communication is still hostile, but much less so than a physical fight. They create conflict unnecessarily bye being rude and defensive. They approach the world and interactions as competitions in which there can only be one winner, so that must be them. They use any type of intimidation available to them to get what they want.

Unsurprisingly, aggressive communicators do not have very much empathy for the people that they are hostile toward, otherwise, they would recognize the harm and their behavior and change it. These people also tend to be on the lower end of the maturity Continuum, because they feel that they are dependent upon others to survive or get their needs met. Because they do not feel empowered, they often do not listen very well or share time, energy, or objects very well.

Aggressive behavioral communication manifests itself in many ways: using intimidating verbal and nonverbal communication, such as physical threats or violence, verbal threats, speaking too loudly, too quickly, or without annunciating to be clearly heard, standing too close, as well as attempting to appear as large and imposing as possible.

Assertive Behavioral Communication

Assertive means to be confident and somewhat forceful in an appropriate manner. Concerning assertive behavioral communication, it is then considered to be a healthy and confident approach to communication. This is a behavior that is direct and respectful, which is perhaps the rarest type of communication.

People who have assertive communication styles generally have a high level of self-worth and empathy, which means they not only have compassion for themselves and their own emotions but also have compassion for those they are communicating with. They can comfortably express their emotions and thoughts as well as hearing the same from others, even if they are different from theirs. They rarely feel the need to manipulate others to get their needs met, preferring instead to maintain their own autonomy, and allowing others to do the same.

Appearing as d highest level of maturity in the continuum, and assertive communicator understands that most situations can and positively for everyone involved and that disagreements can lead to furthering our knowledge and deepening our relationships, rather than devolving into conflicts that cause resentment and relationships. They are often able to set boundaries and communicates clearly when those boundaries have been crossed, usually also allowing for the opportunity to apologize and make it right.

Assertive behavioral communication manifests itself in many ways: being empathetic, actively listening, using positive nonverbal communication, showing interest in others and their thoughts, taking responsibility for their own actions, a good level of impulse control, appropriately sharing time and space with others, being authentic in their relationships, clearly communicating their needs and feelings, as well as being able to admit when they are wrong and apologize.

Passive Behavioral Communication

To be passive is to accept or allow things to happen without responding or resisting. Therefore, when we look at passive behavioral communication, this means these types of communicators do not often express their own emotions or opinions, meaning their needs come last to themselves. This type of Communicator is often referred to as a "people pleaser" for this reason. They would rather make sure that other people's needs are met and emotions are well taken care of before they consider their own, which means they are often in need of something and uncomfortable as a result.

People with a passive style of communication often have such low self-esteem that they do not consider their own emotions and needs to be as important as the people around them. This can be a result of or can simply occur in conjunction with feelings of anxiousness and depression. Because they do not get their needs met, this can often lead to feelings of resentment, which only exacerbates the feelings of inadequacy.

Interestingly enough, passive behavioral communication comes in at the middle level of the maturity Continuum, because while they Have developed past the level of dependency on others, they have moved into a level of Independence where they know they can take care of themselves, but they have a mindset in which they are not worth taking care of. These types of communicators are lacking in the ability to set boundaries and similarly do not communicate when boundaries have been crossed. For this reason, they are often holding onto negative emotions resulting from that.

Passive behavioral communication manifests itself in many ways: using meek verbal and nonverbal communication, minimal eye contact, attempting to take up as little space as possible, using a quiet voice, halting often when speaking, not engaging others and communication, rarely initiating conversations, fidgeting, not speaking up for themselves, and sometimes having emotional outbursts when overwhelmed.

Passive-Aggressive Behavioral Communication

Passive-aggressive is a resistance to something while avoiding it indirectly. It's is a combination of both aggressive communication as well as passive communication. Most commonly it is referred to when there is the level of hostility and confrontational emotions associated with aggression but it is expressed in a passive manner that is very subtle and often underplayed. This type of Behavioral communication is understood to be built from a sense of Low self-esteem and conflict, yet feeling as if they should not express these emotions, which is where the passivity shows up.

Because there is a certain level of deception, which is oftentimes unintentional on their part, their nonverbal communication usually does not match up with their verbal communication. Usually, without even understanding why others will pick up on this and feel that either they are being untruthful or flighty because they are trying to cover up their true emotions with communication, they believe it is acceptable. For this reason, they often do not get their needs met because they neither have the self-esteem to communicate them, in addition to the fact that others are often alienated by their rude behavior.

Much like passive communication, passive-aggressive behavior I'll communication also falls in the second level of the maturity continuum. They have developed past a level of dependency into a level of independent maturity, however, they have learned or decided that the best way to get their needs met is to revert to the first level of maturity, depending on others without using their ability to communicate their needs to others.

Passive-aggressive behavior of communication manifests itself in many ways: the use of sarcasm, backhanded compliments, muttering under one's breath, staying silent when spoken to, attempting to sabotage others, poor nonverbal communication, non-verbal actions that don't match the verbal communication, eye-rolling, unreliability, purposefully obstinate, and chronically forgetful.

Chapter 16
Leadership Skills by Robert Dilts

One of the most popular theories of leadership comes from a researcher and author who has created not only a theory of leadership but a practice that can be measured and applied. Robert Dilts has written many books on the subject, which set the bar for Visionary leadership.

He posits that the ability of a truly great leader is one of the most world-changing events in human history. Specifically, however, his interest is in the Visionary leader, which he argues is the most profound, effective, and positive roles one can have. In fact, he goes on to say that this is actually the only type of leadership that can make change, and therefore should be what leaders strive to become.

Basic Leadership Skills

Dilts Created numerous communication and Leadership models to explain in detail the process of becoming an effective Visionary leader, but some of his most well-cited work is that of the four basic skills of leadership. These address the four types of relationships a leader in counters in their process.

Self-Skills

Self-skills are made up of the actions of their own selves and any given moment. Usually, a Visionary leader has good sales skills, which is what puts them in a position of leading in the first place. They have high emotional intelligence, they have good impulse control, they have critical thinking skills, they have problem-solving skills, and they understand the context of various situations, and act and respond appropriately.

Relational Skills

Next are relational skills, which refer to a leader's ability to relate to others. This is the social skills aspect of emotional intelligence, which encompasses their ability to comfortably communicate, provide motivation for, and generally have positive interactions with others. This is necessary for Visionary leaders because to be a leader you must be effective at getting a team to perform at their highest level, which requires you to relate to them.

Strategic Thinking Skills

Strategic thinking skills refers to the concept of foresight and problem-solving when planning your success in achieving an end goal. This is a more advanced skill that requires emotional intelligence, but they are not necessarily dependent upon each other, nor does one lead to the other. Understandably, the ability to think strategically is a calculating type of skill, but when it comes to leadership, it requires that you understand the abilities and strong suits of your team members to choose the best roles for each person an order who creates the best outcome.

Systemic Thinking Skills

Systemic thinking skills refers to the leader's ability to contextualize where they are at that moment. Now that they have established what the end goal is and who is best suited to address each aspect of the process, the leader must establish the enumerated process in and of itself. The system in which everyone will contribute and how they well no if they are succeeding. In a work environment, a lot of the system is already established oh, so very little thought is put into it. However, a Leader's ability to recognize whether the status quo system is the best option or not is crucial, and how to apply the right system is truly visionary.

Perceptual Positions

He also discovered the three perceptual positions that a great Visionary leader must take to increase a team's chance at success. This is a combination of having the creativity to create a vision for the team, the Strategic problem-solving skills to put a plan into action, and the logical distance to step back from a plan to figure out what its flaws are.

Dreamer

The first of a Visionary leader's creative process is to be a dreamer. This is where you have all the freedom in the world and outside of it. You should be thinking outside of the box. There is no ceiling or limitations to what is possible, so you can let your ideas flow freely. This is where truly innovative creations materialize. This is the time in which you want to imagine your ideal end goal.

Realist

The follow up to the dreamer's vision is to then imagine it in the real world. Can you see it and feel it? Is it possible with the resources currently available? Is there a market or a reason for it? Is there enough time to figure out how to make the vision a reality, and do you have the team necessary to do it? This is also the part of the process in which you do you start strategizing and planning. This is the time in which you start to implement and define the road you will take to reach the end goal.

Critic

Finally, before you get too far into a process or committed to the outcome, you must attempt to look into the future and predict where things are likely to go wrong. This is the part of the journey in which you decide if the effort is worth it. You must attempt to measure the expected payoff in comparison to the expected effort. This is perhaps the most difficult part of the process for many people because it requires a level of detachment that's many people struggle to achieve. You must look at and idea impersonally and as if it were someone else's bye being objective. This is the time in which you will evaluate and reassess to give feedback along your journey toward the end goal.

Practicing Effective Leadership Communication Skills

Now understanding Dilts' theories on basic leadership skills and perceptual positions for Visionary leaders, we can apply these to effective communication skills.

When communicating with your team, first you have to know what message you want to give to them. This can include any sort of meetings or informative messages you have to communicate with them to achieve your goals, but this can also be applied whenever you are talking or interacting with members of your team. This means that if you are consciously sending important information, then you need to know what information you hope they retain from it.

This also means you will want to consider what the best medium in communicating that information is, the tone of how you want them to understand your emotions, how you want this message to affect them and their emotions, as well as what type of relationship status you want to have with your team members. Even if you are simply making small talk unrelated to work, you should have an idea of all of these answers and your head.

Next, you have to actually deliver your message. This means verbally and non-verbally. During this process, you should use your emotional intelligence to make sure you are communicating what & in the way that you intended to, as well as being conscious of your team's emotional state and engagement.

Third, you have to figure out if your team members received the message that you intended them to receive. You need to know if they understood what you wanted to convey, not only concerning the specific message, but also concerning all of the aspects mentioned in the first step.

Finally, you need to reflect on this communication process. If the message your team received is not in line with the message you intended to send, you need to figure out where the disconnect is in that process. This can even be so drastic that you recognize the difference between your intended message and the message you actually gave. Oftentimes, this is when you learn best the importance and effect of nonverbal communication.

It is important to remember that every person and type of leader is difference, as well as every team. Depending upon your goals, tasks, or interactions, how you approach effective leadership communication skills will vary from interaction to interaction. Of course, there is also Defector of each member of your team having different levels of emotional intelligence and learning better in different styles. It is your task to make sure that you, to a certain degree, accommodate everyone's communication and learning styles, to an appropriate level.

You will also likely notice that the members of your team probably tend to lean toward one of the three types of perceptual positions previously discussed. You can also use this knowledge to your advantage to help your team know when each perceptual input is most valuable, as well as when it can hinder communication and teamwork.

Chapter 17
The 5 Essential Qualities of
a Great Leader

Clarity

The First Quality that is essential four great leaders is the clarity. That is because the vision and the end goal must be clear for your team to understand why they should follow you and how they can follow you. Without clarity, it could be argued that you are not a leader.

Beyond the necessity to establish that you are leading to something, this quality is essential in becoming a Visionary and transformational leader. This is because when you have a Clear Vision that you communicate clearly to others, from there they will be able to make their own decisions as to whether or not they want to follow you. This allows them to check in with their own internal motivations and find reasons that are important to them that will allow them to buy into your vision and truly dedicate themselves to the success of the team.

This is an especially difficult quality to maintain for many people because they lack the Strategic and systemic skills necessary to create a clear path to a Clear Vision. The Rarity of this quality will make you seem like that much more of an attractive leader because it is so hard to come across.

This includes everything from knowing what the end goal is, knowing the path to get there, all the way down to understanding how you are perceived by others on a micro-level. This requires a very high level of emotional intelligence because you are going to be communicating quite nearly at all times.

From establishing systems and setting boundaries for yourself and your team, all the way to being seen as someone authentic and inspiring, you have to know yourself and your communication styles so well to be able to strike a balance that is effective for you and each member of your team. A group cannot successfully reach their end goal if they do not know what is expected of them, where they can find support, or how they should proceed, which is where your ability to provide Clarity at all times along the process will become crucial.

Decisiveness

The ability to be decisive and commit to a decision is crucial four a high-quality leader because it lets your team members build a level of trust with you. If you are constantly second-guessing and redirecting your course, they will not be able to trust that you know where they are going or how to get them there. By being decisive and consistent with your decisions, you instill a level of knowledge and faith in your vision. Not only that, but you show them that you trust their abilities and skills in fulfilling your vision.

It is important to note that decisiveness does not mean impulsiveness or bullheadedness. It incorporates a level of expertise and knowledge that allows for the right decision to come forth easily but also knowing that there are usually many right decisions, so the only wrong decision is to flip-flop between them. It is also different from being stubborn because it is not about ignoring information to stay the course, but rather knowing that obstacles will come up in every journey, and trusting the process will see you through the difficulties.

Decisiveness eliminates procrastination, which is often simply a product of fear. If you do not take action, you cannot move forward. While thinking and considering is certainly an important part of any process, if you get stuck there for too long, you will think yourself out of taking any action at all. If you allow too much deliberation and a collaborative or group setting, this can destroy teamwork and inspiration toward the vision. Your efforts mustn't become paralyzed by so many options that you can't make a decision.

This also includes the ability to admit when a decision was wrong because making a wrong decision is more fruitful and educational then not making any decision. Oftentimes, teams and individuals learn as they go, which requires a level of trust both from the leader trusting that the team members will step up, as well as on the team members' part trusting that the leader has not gotten them in over their head. This process establishes a deeper level of connection, trust, and commitment because they will have journeyed and grown together.

Courage

The quality of Courage as a leader presents itself in so many forms, yet it might be the most difficult of all qualities to possess and maintain. This requires a level of confidence and trust in yourself and your knowledge to know when risks are worth the payoff in comparison to their likelihood of failing their succeeding and concerning their repercussions. The ability to take risks is something that every leader is going to have to do if they want to be Visionary and transformational, and this requires a high level of Courage.

The great thing about being a good leader, though, is that not only do you inspire courage in your team members, but if you have done your job well, your team members will expire courage in you, because those risks are proven to be mitigated by your great team.

The fact that you are leading, rather than simply being in a signed manager, means that you absolutely have the skills to be a great leader and therefore you should feel comfortable in choosing courageousness over safety from time to time. the confidence comes from truly putting your emotional intelligence to use for yourself, recognizing the times that you have succeeded, the things you've learned from every failure, and the compassion to know that both of those are important in growing. Because of that, you should be confident in your ability to fulfill your role as a leader and Inspire courageousness in your team members.

Part of every journey toward an end goal includes many steps along the way that are undesirable, tedious, or downright unpleasant. That doesn't mean they aren't necessary or that the goal isn't worth striving for even though you have to do those tasks. So, in that way, you as a leader will always be making decisions that other people do not like. It takes courage to make that decision.

This is a type of upward spiraling quality, because every time you act courageously, you build your Reserves for future courageous actions.

Another aspect of being courageous as a leader is simply and your inspiration of your team members. Because everyone wants to contribute positively and uniquely to their end goal, and this is done through various internal motivating factors of their own, you are truly instigating something inside of another person that you do not have control of. When that happens, you are encouraging them to make bold choices, be creative, and choose courageousness themselves.

Passion

Perhaps the most inspiring quality a leader can possess is that a passion. It is a combination of bringing your authentic self to your interactions with others and your work, along with your expertise and vision. This is an advanced quality that few people possess, and even fewer can effectively utilize and communicate. When you can bring a passion to your team, it shows them that you are committed, which tells them you will support them in their journey, because you want success as much as they do. It also lets them know that your end goal is something worth striving for and achieving.

Your passion as a leader is something that is an internal motivating factor. It is deeply important to you, and external factors do not and cannot affect it. This is a great opportunity to act as a role model in that way to your team members by helping them to see the opportunities for their motivation. Often, it can also inspire passion in your team members, which acts as a positive spiral of self-fulfilling motivation back and forth.

It is also effective as a leadership quality because it makes a huge difference in the energy that you bring as a leader to your team. When you are passionate about something, it is a type of positivity that creates an inspiring attitude and uplifting environment to work in.

Humility

Finally, an important leadership quality is humility. While we have already established that you should be confident as a leader that is not mutually exclusive from being humble. Part of having high emotional intelligence is being able to admit when you are wrong, apologizing, and learning from your mistakes.

As already mentioned, it's important to be decisive, but sometimes you are going to make the wrong decision. However, because making any decision is better than stagnating, there is always a lesson to learn in straying down an incorrect path. It is your job to learn as much as possible as quickly as possible, to put your leadership skills to the test.

Oftentimes, however, criticism and learning opportunities are going to come very harshly or with little Compassion or consideration for your feelings. That is okay because as a great leader, you already have high emotional intelligence and you should be able to manage your emotions to truly hear what you need to learn. Rather than becoming defensive or closing off, you should have the skills and ability to truly thank the person or thing that is teaching you an important lesson.

This also means you find your own opportunities aside from failures to learn as much as you can. No one person can know everything, so remaining humble will keep you a Perpetual student, which will serve well as you try to grow as a leader, as well as showing your team members that you are trustworthy and compassionate.

Chapter 18
Positive Communication Style

Be an Active Listener

Perhaps the most important part of a positive communication style is active listening. Not only because you are showing the other person that you were engaged, but because the act of active listening means that you truly are engaged, therefore you are truly hearing and understanding what the other person is communicating.

This is a skill that requires practice and you can improve upon effort. It requires using most if not all of your senses, and it demands your attention. It is not a passive process that happens to you, but rather is a practice that you actively participate in on an ongoing basis. This includes hearing and understanding verbal communication, as well as their nonverbal communication.

Some other things you can do consciously to be an active listener is to give some verbal feedback such as saying "yes" or "I understand" or other words or phrases that tell the other person you are on the same page has them. This encourages them to continue communicating because you are interested. Another great way to stay engaged is to be curious and ask questions. Whether these are clarifying questions or questions that are related but take the conversation in a different direction, you are showing that's this is something that connects with you. This can also include reflecting on what was said, asking them to reflect on what they've said, and even offering your summary of what they said to confirm that you correctly understood what they've said.

Open Body Language

Of course, it is important to show with your body language that you are open to communication and you want to engage with other people. Because so much information is communicated non-verbally, partly due to the fact that are non verbals often happen unconsciously, and partly due to the fact that we have so many more senses to take in information

Beyond just our ears, this is perhaps the most difficult to change in a person because we tend to have very strong habits.

as discussed in chapter 10, there are a myriad of things to focus on and consider when discussing body language and nonverbal communication. But when it comes to maintaining positive communication Styles and open body language, you can let a lot of it come naturally. You should show that you are active listening, to communicate with the other person that you are engaged. However, oftentimes, your non-verbal actions are unconscious when you truly are actively listening. you will use nonverbal cues such as smiling, using eye contact, adjusting your posture to lean in and sit up, mirroring their body language, and avoiding distractions. These are all actions that you will naturally take without even thinking about it if you truly are engaged.

Adjusting to Various Communication Styles

With all of the knowledge you have acquired and improvements you've made in your emotional intelligence, this is the aspect where you have to put it all to the test. We do not learn these things because there is one right way to communicate or one correct way to act. Rather, we learn these things so that we can ring this knowledge to others in the way that we interact with them. We have various tools in our tool belt that allow us to adjust according to the situation and two individuals' different communication styles.

Rather than being rigid in our communication style, for instance, thinking that because we have all of this knowledge, this is the way everyone should be, we are going to use our emotional intelligence to be compassionate and understand that everyone has a different perspective and way of communicating. Exactly what you do to adjust will depend upon your communication style and the communication style of the person you are trying to communicate with. However, across the board, there are a few things that are applicable no matter the situation.

The first thing you want to consider is who you are communicating with, especially if there are enumerated roles, positions, or hierarchical processes to follow. Choosing the appropriate tone is crucial, but it depends on your context. Next, you can decide what medium or channel is best to communicate through. Whether that be in person, over the phone, an email, or some other way, all of these alter tea effectiveness of communication and also have their effect on the tone.

Showing Fairness

Showing fairness as a leader is important, and it incorporates aspects of Concepts we've learned throughout this book so far. Most obviously, the idea of being fair requires a level of objectivity, which means getting distance from a situation or a thought to not take it personally. This is a part of having high emotional intelligence, because it requires that you are humble enough to consider and recognize that your emotions might be in control, from time to time.

It is also especially applicable when we are considering the behavioral communication styles, because of the four types, only one is truly able to be fair. Because of maladaptive learned behaviors that contribute to the passive, passive-aggressive, and aggressive behavioral communication Styles, none of these allow for very much perspective or communicated boundaries. Assertive communication, however, allows for learning and growing, along with the self-esteem necessary to create and maintain fair and balanced boundaries.

When it comes to being a good leader, showing fairness to your team members is crucial for them to trust you and the process. If they are receiving mixed messages about this system or your strategy to get them to their end goal, they will lose motivation, because the outcomes and rewards are not based on a system that makes sense.

Utilizing Feedback

Being able to recognize when you are receiving feedback as a leader, and then especially utilizing that feedback is often perceived as a difficulty or a struggle, but when you recognized it for the growing and learning opportunity that it is, you might very well change your view of it for the positive.

It requires being humble to receive feedback of any kind and at any level. If you keep in mind that you want to learn and grow, however, this will become easier. You must learn how to separate the message from the delivery. This is especially difficult when the person you are receiving feedback from does not have high emotional intelligence, and therefore they are not especially compassionate or considerate about your Feelings. That being said, there is still something that they can teach you, even if they present it very rudely.

Much like assessing hour communication process and determining if our intended message was communicated effectively and received the way we wanted, we can use any and all types of feedback in this same reflection process. When we get feedback that communicates to us that our message was unclear, convoluted, or entirely misunderstood, rather than focusing on how the other person could have mistaken the message, it is actually an opportunity for us to turn inward yet again to determine how our actions can better serve our message.

Engaging and Motivating

One very effective way to maintain positive communication that engages and motivates your team is almost always completely overlooked but will have a profound impact. This is scheduling meetings that you do not have a particular outcome in mind. By simply scheduling times, this can be as little as five or 10 minutes, with each individual on your team, this allows them to bring up any topics they need to discuss without you driving the rains. This shows them that you are interested in their feedback and want to help them in any way you can.

That meeting can include, or you can simply use this technique in brake type settings, of getting to know your team members personally. Everyone has a life outside of work, and ideally, that life is more important to them and you then this career goal. So, if you can get to know the person behind the work team member you will have a better understanding of how and why they are engaged and motivated. This also helps improve your emotional intelligence and allows them to see a more personal side of you, which allows your authentic self to shine through.

Personalize Your Communication

When you understand your team members better, you will become more effective at personalizing your communication with each one of them individually. While bosses of old would have thought that this is a waste of effort and that everyone should get on their page, as transformational and Visionary leaders, we recognize that it's in our best interest to meet our team members were they are there to help them grow in advance, rather than losing out on a good employee for whom we cannot adapt to.

Rather than thinking about personalizing your communication as a negative aspect or something extra you have to do, you can think of it as practicing and exercising your emotional intelligence. It is truly an Adept skill that will pay off tenfold when you can confidently say that you understand the best way to engage, clarify, motivate, and get results from each individual that is on your team, even win every person has a different communication style and behavioral communication style, not to mention varying levels of emotional intelligence themselves. Your ability to contextualize and go with the flow is a very enviable and profitable skill set.

Clarify Your Communication

Since you already know how to measure if your intended message was received accurately by the people you were communicating with, you should have a good understanding of how to clarify your communication with them. It is important to note that there will always be some fluidity between your intended message and the received message because that is the nature of communication. Rather than deeming your communication skills a success or failure based upon the exact accurate reception of your message, you should instead focus on getting the important points across in whatever way works best for the receiver.

one way you can do this is to try to summarize your message in one succinct sentence, and ask them if they can reiterate in their own words what they understand you are message to be. In this way you allow them to process the information in their own way, which allows you to make sure that it makes sense to them while also validating and confirming that you are not micromanaging their thoughts. You can also follow up with them after the fact to confirm that they still recall what you consider to be an important message. This not only gives them a time to mentally take in, process, and expound upon your message, but it also tells them that you are open to ongoing check-ins and feedback, which lets them know you support their work.

Chapter 19
Mistakes Leaders Make

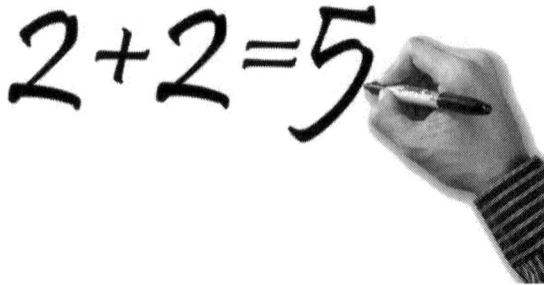

$$2+2=5$$

Failure to Delegate

When is the most demoralizing problem a team can have is a leader who fails to delegate. This is a leader who doesn't trust their team to solve problems or get tasks done, and often these are relatively menial tasks that should be able to be accomplished by anyone on the team. These types of leaders are bad at time management and most likely are also poor communicators. This will lead to the leader being completely burnt out and possibly having an emotional outburst when things get too overwhelming.

one red flag concerning delegating is a Leader's willingness to teach their employees new skills needed to accomplish their own work. The amount of effort it takes to train someone is Tiny in comparison to the amount of time a leader will save by delegating that task to someone else rather than doing it themselves for the rest of their career. Whether this is because the leader doesn't trust the employee's ability, the leader thinks that teaching their employee this skill will make themselves less valuable, they are bad at prioritizing and time management, or they simply don't want to make the effort, these can all lead to the same result of failing to delegate.

Neglecting to Provide Feedback

Everyone just wants to know that they are doing a good job, whether that's at work, at home, or in their Hobbies. Since we spend so much of our adult life at work, as Leaders we should make sure that our employees and team members no that we appreciate them and their efforts. A very common mistake many leaders make is neglecting to provide feedback to their employees. This means both positively and negatively. Many leaders simply don't take the time to check-in with their employees.

Obviously, one of the most profound ways we can improve Morale on our team is by celebrating victories, whether large or small. Most likely, your team members are doing a great job most of the time. While we, of course, expect that to be the norm, that doesn't mean that it should go unnoticed. Especially if you have ever had a poor working experience, you should know firsthand that having a great team is a luxury and a privilege. So, any opportunity you get to point out your team's successes or individual member's contributions, you should do so both privately and publicly.

Conversely, if someone on your team is not meeting basic standards, they should have a clear understanding of that. Not only should they have clear expectations for what they need to do, they should know if they are meeting those, how they can meet those expectations, where they are falling short, and what follow up they will get if they do not meet those expectations.

Avoiding Conflict

Part of the reason many leaders neglect to provide feedback is that they want to avoid conflict. No one is especially comfortable with conflict, but an important part of being a leader in helping your team members achieve the objective. It should be noted that if you are providing feedback to a team member, while that feedback might be that they are not meeting expectations, it should still be done with a positive attitude and an optimistic tone. Going into any situation with the expectation that it will become a conflict will almost certainly guarantee that it will.

Ideally, if you have practiced and made an effort to improve your emotional intelligence, even if your employee is upset during an interaction, you should have a pretty good idea of how to diffuse the situation to prevent it from becoming an emotional outburst. If, however, you avoid difficult conversations in an attempt to avoid conflict, this shows that you have not worked on your emotional intelligence. Bye going into difficult conversations with the mindset of getting on the same page and clarifying how you got to the situation, you will make it a more comfortable conversation rather than a one-sided dressing down of your employee, which will almost certainly cause problems.

Failing to Set Goals and Define Vision

We already know how important it is to set a goal and Define a vision as a leader, yet so many people neglect this aspect, and their team pays for it drastically. Without having an end goal in mind, your daily tasks are without purpose and often end up Meandering all over the board. This is especially true when difficult decisions must be made. If there is no vision, you have no Direction in making a difficult decision.

When a leader fails to set goals or to find their Vision, there is absolutely no way that their team members or employees can get behind their efforts. They simply don't know what the efforts are! You need your employees to buy into the vision for them to find their internal motivation, which will Propel your team forward. If your team members don't know what the end goal is, they will not go above and beyond or even anywhere close to their maximum effort for the team. When they lack vision, they also lack intellectual stimulation, which leads to creativity and innovation.

Reactivity Instead of Proactivity

These days, many leaders find themselves overworked, overwhelmed, and understaffed. That leads them to work too many hours, not being caught up, and constantly reacting to events that occur, rather than being proactive and getting out in front of any problems that might arise. While this may seem like the only way to survive by putting out fires, this is a very common mistake that can be overcome.

Of course, you need the ability to react on your toes, make quick and smart decisions, re-tool, and redirect when things go awry, and innovate Solutions. However, rather than that being the only thing you do, you should also be able to predict and proactively make decisions about what you see coming down the pipeline. When you can get this kind of grasp and distance on your work, you and your team members will feel more in control of your daily workload as well as your ability to accomplish the tasks on your route to your end goal.

This does require taking some time out to think about issues you are having and if they are preventable or if there are patterns in them. This may mean that you need to schedule a time to think about it without interruption, either by yourself or as a team. It takes a level of foresight, patience, and Trust in the process.

Forgetting Humility

Too many leaders today and throughout the ages have lacked humility. Understandably, an aggressive personality type tends to become leaders more frequently, but that doesn't make it an effective communication Style. The assertive behavioral communication style is the healthy and emotionally intelligent way to Be an Effective leader that is both confident as well as humble.

Because many liters are used to having a lot of power, they mistakenly think that they are entitled to being in charge or having power, that they are always right, that today can and should micromanage others, and that they should have control over others, including in manipulative ways. These are all incorrect. A Team cannot function successfully in this type of environment. Because it takes every single member on a team to achieve a goal, leaders must remember that they are simply one part of the team and not the overarching reason for the team's success. To celebrate your team's victories and not claiming them for your own is an important function of being a leader.

Misunderstanding Motivation

Of course, we all go to work to get a paycheck. This certainly is a motivating factor for 99% of the workforce. However, chances are it is not the main motivating factor and why your employees are in your company performing their jobs. We are all complicated, nuanced, and intelligent humans who need to be fulfilled both mentally, physically, intellectually, and spiritually. While earning money to take care of their Primal needs is important, almost everyone has many options when it comes to exactly where they earn that paycheck. If you take the time out to understand the motivation of your employees, you will be light years ahead of the competition.

There are three things that everyone wants when they go to work because they spend so much of their waking adult life there. They want to know that they are doing the correct thing and that their job matters in the grand scheme of things. They want to know that things are fair and equal, and both promotions and emotions are clarified in a way that they understand when they will be either punished or celebrated. They also simply want to have a pleasant time while they are at work, enjoy the company of their peers, and feel safe and comfortable as a team.

Misunderstanding Your Position

To be a transformational Visionary leader, you must understand your position within the team to get everyone's best efforts. Keeping the above in mind, many leaders make the mistake that they have to drastically change themselves, their team, or their definition of what a leader does.

Being a leader does not mean that you have to be the one person with all of the answers, the one person who makes all of the decisions, the person who is always right, or the person with the most experience. While you certainly could be any or all of those things, your position is not to get your ego stroked by making your team members kowtow to your expertise. To that same end, your position is not there to achieve a goal at the expense of your employees' well-being. It might seem like you can expedite the process of reaching your goal by abusing and mistreating your employees, but while that short-term solution might get you a small success, in the long-term, that will backfire and result in an end-goal failure.

on the flip side, your position is not to make sure everything keeps going exactly as it has been without any conflict or growth. While it is nice to be liked as a leader, if you are not inspiring your team members to grow, learn, and innovate, you aren't really leading.

Losing Faith in Your Abilities

When you, as a leader, no longer have faith or trust in your own ability as a leader, that is something your team members can absolutely feel themselves. This is something that can happen when you have lost sight of the vision for the team. When you aren't sure where you are going, you can very easily feel inadequate in your ability to reach the end goal. This could also be the effect of being inauthentic in your promises. If you have committed your team to reach a goal that you do not feel a level of Integrity about reaching, you will start to question everything about yourself as a leader. That also includes any promises you make to your employees about what you aren't sure that you can deliver on.

Many times, however, leaders lose face in their abilities because they are out of touch with their team members. When you isolate yourself and work in a bubble without any communication or feedback, you have no idea where you stand concerning them or your end goal. By making sure that you are practicing your emotional intelligence and keeping yourself in the loop with your team members, you will re-energize your efforts.

Forgetting that you're a Team

Some leaders have been leaders for so long that they have forgotten what it's like to take Direction, have a leader, and be lower on the totem pole. When you don't have very many peers or when you are not working very closely with people of your same position, it's easy to forget that you are on a team. It is crucial to your leadership abilities that you always keep this in mind.

Even as a leader, there should be two-way communication at all times that keep you and them in the loop about updates, as well as the possibility that you have things to learn from them and that you can be wrong. If you fail to do these things, you will find your team becoming less and less productive, effective, and motivated. If you need to get back in touch with your team, not only should you make sure that all lines of communication are open, and they feel comfortable communicating with you, but you should take time out to get in the weeds with them and remind yourself of the roles each of them plays in achieving your team's overall goal.

Chapter 20
Practical Ways to Use Emotional Intelligence to Improve Your Life

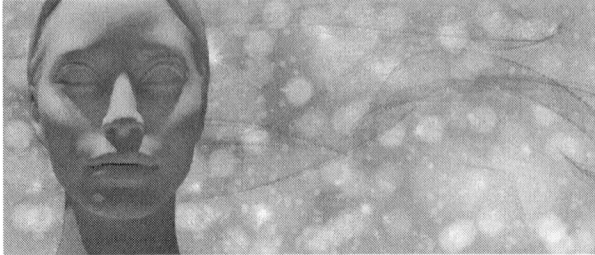

Self-Management and Relationship Management

When you have high emotional intelligence, you are much more confident in your abilities to manage your own emotions but also to interact with others. This means that you have practiced and successfully managed your impulse control, so you feel totally in control of your own life, rather than being jerked around by sudden impulses. This can often lead to more positive self-perception, confidence, and self-esteem. When you truly understand that you are in control of your life, thoughts, and emotions, you feel happier.

This also means that you have developed a level of trust within yourself that translates into proving to others that you are trustworthy with them. This shows that you have a good moral compass, and you are conscientious in your thought process.

You have experience in difficult situations that you have successfully overcome, and you can confidently tell that to others. It gives you the ability to adapt to change because you are flexible with things that happened to you because you know you are in control of yourself.

All of this confidence also gives you the ability to excel in social interactions. Because you come from a place of positivity and flexibility, you can use this to start conversations with other people. This is truly an art form that is losing Steam with every technological advancement, so the more you do it and the better you are at it, the more you will stand out as emotionally intelligent and as someone who others want to talk with.

Putting Emotional Intelligence to Good Use in the Workplace

There are countless ways you can successfully use emotional intelligence to improve in the workplace. Perhaps the most difficult yet most effective way to do so is to honestly take stock of your own strengths and weaknesses at work. Rather than using this as an opportunity to tear yourself down, this is simply an assessment of things you do well, and therefore can find ways to do more of that at work, as well as areas that you can improve upon, so when you get feedback in those areas, you can truly take note of those.

It is also important that you find ways to healthily and appropriately deal with any stress that might come up at work. Making sure that you have a balance in your life to take time outside of work to enjoy Hobbies or get physical exercise in are great ways to help mitigate stressors at work. This also includes the ability to control any emotional outbursts that might happen while at work. Using your self-regulation skills, you can stay cool under pressure rather than letting your impulse control off the hook.

You will also find that you naturally search for positive things that happened while at work, as well as finding your internal motivation when you apply your emotional intelligence in the workplace. By focusing on why you took the job, what you enjoy about your job, the positive outcome you have in your team and in your company, as well as the underlying positive impact your company has on the world, not only will you continually refill your Reserves of motivation when times get tough, but you will also rub off on your coworkers.

When you show up to work every day and utilize your emotional intelligence to create a healthy and positive workplace for you and your team members, this can actually help them become more emotionally intelligent as well. Because you have the perspective necessary to have a healthy view of your work, this will help you choose to be respectful and assertive in creating, setting, and enforcing boundaries around work. By clarifying your boundaries and expectations, not only will you benefit from this, but your team members will have a role model of how to set their boundaries, as well as having a level of trust with you that they know when and how to communicate with you.

Using Emotional Intelligence as a Guide in Decision Making

An important part of using emotional intelligence to become a great leader is its effect on decision-making. We have already established that both are important for a good leader, but how do they apply to each other. Well, it is a matter of using your emotional intelligence to recognize what information is and is not important when making a decision. This is going to change and be dependent upon each individual situation, but there are a few ways that emotional intelligence helps.

Being able to control our impulses is important when making decisions because, as we discussed earlier, some impulses that we are unaware of lead us to take actions without a single thought. Other times, we get so wrapped up in overwhelming emotions that we make rash decisions to Simply eliminate the negative emotion we no longer want to feel. Conversely, sometimes we are so wrapped up in positive overwhelming emotions that we make decisions that we cannot backup or fulfill in the future. All of these are things that can be mitigated by improving our emotional intelligence.

When it comes to the workplace, sometimes it feels like there are split-second decisions that have to be made, fires are put out, and emergencies that happen very quickly. However, by flexing or emotional intelligence muscle, we will be able to put some distance between the event and our emotions, which allow us to determine if our instincts are simply impulses to mitigate negative emotions in the short-term or if they are truly going to be successful long-term Solutions to the issue. This doesn't mean that we no longer feel emotions, it simply means that we acknowledge the emotions we are feeling and logically assess if they apply to the moment and if so if they can help us make the right choice rather than taking full control over all of the choices.

Using Emotional Intelligence to Improve Your Communication

Oftentimes, when you come in contact with someone who is emotionally intelligent, you are drawn to them and want to communicate with them more than with others. This is because they are using their skills to tell you that you are important, and what you have to say is worth listening to. You can use your emotional intelligence to be that person to others.

By using your active listening skills, you are conveying to others that they have important things to say that you need to hear, they are worth your time, they are valuable, and that you are engaged with them. At a time when technological advancements make our attention span get shorter and shorter with every passing day, your ability to give your attention to one person for an extended amount of time is immensely attractive and flattering.

When you can successfully summarize and reiterate in your own words the message that they just communicated to you, this reinforces your interest in them. It also confirms for them that they are communicating clearly, as well as the fact that you are truly listening and understand them. Everyone just wants to be understood, so the better you are at conveying this to them, d more they will trust and appreciate you.

This also helps you find ways to share parts of yourself with them. When you can connect someone else's message or personal information to that of your own, not only does that allow you to engage yourself in the conversation, but it also helps you to bring your authentic and true self to the table. Everyone wants to know that they aren't alone in the world, and anytime they can be told that they share something with another person, this fulfills a deep-seated need within them.

Using Emotional Intelligence to Have Better Relationships with People

When many people feel defensive, misunderstood, or undervalued, they come to two interactions with others from a place of negativity. That is understandable when that is the norm for much of their communication. However, to break out of the victim mentality and truly use our emotional intelligence to have better relationships with people, we have to forget about any negative patterns we are expecting from others and move forward courageously expecting a positive outcome.

A great way to go about this is by simply assuming that other people have good intentions. This is especially true when there is a misunderstanding, a ball was dropped, or during any difficult interactions at work. If an employee is not meeting expectations, rather than starting the conversation expecting a conflict or assuming that they are purposefully failing, assume that there is something important that you don't know about yet.

Most often, that turns out to be the case. Because most employees don't want to let their personal lives interfere with their professional work, there are many reasons why they might keep information from you, yet you do see the effects negatively impacting their work. This also allows you to hear the perspective of the other people on your team, which keeps you in the loop and reinforces the fact that you are open to feedback from them. This allows communication to flow freely in both directions, which improves morale exponentially.

When you go into a conversation assuming the best intentions, it will be obvious to the other person you are communicating with, and it will establish a level of trust between the two of you. You are showing compassion and empathy without the other person having to prove anything to you or share more than they are comfortable with. This will result in a profound level of loyalty and positivity on their part.

Emotional Intelligence as an Important Tool for Connections in Healthcare

One topic that comes up over and over again when it comes to Health Care is the lack of bedside manner that's patience desire. This, of course, is simply another way to rephrase emotional intelligence. If a physician or healthcare provider has high emotional intelligence, then they have a good bedside manner. Oftentimes, health care providers seem cold, uncommunicative, and lack a level of empathy for their patients, which leaves the average person feeling lost, confused, and not cared for.

Because Health Care Providers routinely deal with illnesses, problems, and people all day every day, it's understandable that they lose a certain sense of personal perspective. However, for each individual that they are dealing with, their health issue is, in fact, deeply and truly, their entire life. So, there can be a disconnect between the health care provider and the patient. This is a lack of emotional intelligence due to the health care provider, not using empathy for their patients.

A good way to begin building up apathy is to start with Rapport and building a personal connection. While it may not always assist the healthcare provider in pinpointing the problem and, therefore the solution to the health issue, it is still necessary for providing care for a patient. At the very least, it will lead to a level of trust that results in the patient being more forthcoming and participating in the solutions they are offered.

A great way to apply your emotional intelligence and a healthcare setting is to be communicative to let them know what is happening so that they can feel a level of control around their health. This means explaining the behavior that is either causing a problem or providing the solution. Explain the effect and impact that behavior is having on the person's health. Clarify your expectations of what they should do next and request that they follow through with it. Finally, you can outline the results and positive outcomes they will receive by following your solution.

Building Resilience with Emotional Intelligence

Perhaps the most important thing you can do with your emotional intelligence is to use it to help build your resilience. Just like emotional intelligence, it is a muscle that can be built up and must be used to maintain it. This is best understood by your ability to empathize with yourself and have compassion.

By being able to put the situation into perspective, this will help you to maintain a level of composure around difficulties. Being self-aware and managing your emotions can help take the sting off immediately. However, sometimes, we have obstacles that truly stick with us for a long time. In those cases, it requires an ongoing amount of self-compassion and gentleness that many people aren't used to practicing with themselves.

If you can first recognize the situation that caused the trauma or difficult events, that will help you to find solutions to overcoming and being resilient. When you understand that it is normal that your thoughts and emotions influence the actions and decisions you make, you can begin to overcome the overwhelming issue you were having. Next you we'll need to do some self-assessment in recognizing what coping mechanisms you currently use and how effective they are. Some great ways to deal with stress are by communicating with others, whether that is a trusted friend or a professional, such as a therapist.

Conclusion

Thank you for making it through to the end of *Emotional Intelligence for Leadership: The Ultimate Guide to Improve Your Ability to Manage People and Your Social Skills. Boost Your EQ, Self-Discipline and Self Confidence (EQ 2.0)*, let's hope it was informative and able to provide you with all of the tools you need to achieve your goals whatever they may be.

The next step is to simply put this knowledge into practice. The great thing about this book is that it contains absolutely everything you need. The only thing you need to do next is to use it. This is an ongoing learning process for the rest of your life, so you can refer back to this book as often as you need. As you become more emotionally intelligent, and many of these skills become habits and more natural to you, you will begin to advance through the more nuanced and difficult aspects this book outlines for you.

You will be amazed to find the positive changes that occur in your life when you put the effort toward improving your emotional intelligence, especially in the workplace as a leader. You will find your relationships flow much easier, your team works much more productively and effectively, and you are succeeding in meeting goals much easier than before.

Finally, if you found this book useful in any way, a review on Amazon is always appreciated! I appreciate your time, and best of luck with your personal and professional development.

Printed in Great Britain
by Amazon